YOUR DEATH

paintings of
Ali Bazmandegan

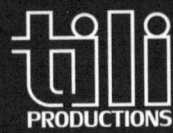

ISBN
978-0-9855565-5-6

YOUR DEATH

Nothing could stop you.
Not the best day. Not the quiet. Not the ocean rocking.
You went on with your dying.
Not the trees
Under which you walked, not the trees that shaded you.
Not the doctor
Who warned you, the white-haired young doctor who saved you once.
You went on with your death.
Nothing could stop you. Not your son. Not your daughter
Who fed you and made you into a child again.
Not your son who thought you would live forever.
Not the wind that shook your lapels.
Not the stillness that offered itself to your motion.
Not your shoes that grew heavier.
Not your eyes that refused to look ahead.
Nothing could stop you.
You sat in your room and stared at the city
And went on with your death.
You went to work and let the cold enter your clothes.
You let blood seep into your socks.
Your face turned white.
Your voice cracked in two.
You leaned on your cane.
But nothing could stop you.
Not your friends who gave you advice.
Not your son. Not your daughter who watched you grow small.
Not fatigue that lived in your sighs.
Not your lungs that would fill with water.

Not your sleeves that carried the pain of your arms.
Nothing could stop you.
You went on with your death.
When you played with children you went on with your death.
When you sat down to eat,
When you woke up at night, wet with tears, your body sobbing,
You went on with your dying.
Nothing could stop you.
Not the past.
Not the future with its good weather.
Not the view from your window, the view of the graveyard.
Not the city. Not the terrible city with its wooden buildings.
Not defeat. Not success.
You did nothing but go on with your death.
You put your watch to your ear.
You felt yourself slipping.
You lay on the bed.
You folded your arms over your chest and you dreamed of the world
without you,
Of the space under the trees,
Of the space in your room,
Of the spaces that would now be empty of you,
And you went on with your death.
Nothing could stop you.
Not your breathing. Not your life.
Not the life you wanted.
Not the life you had.
Nothing could stop you.

MARK STRAND

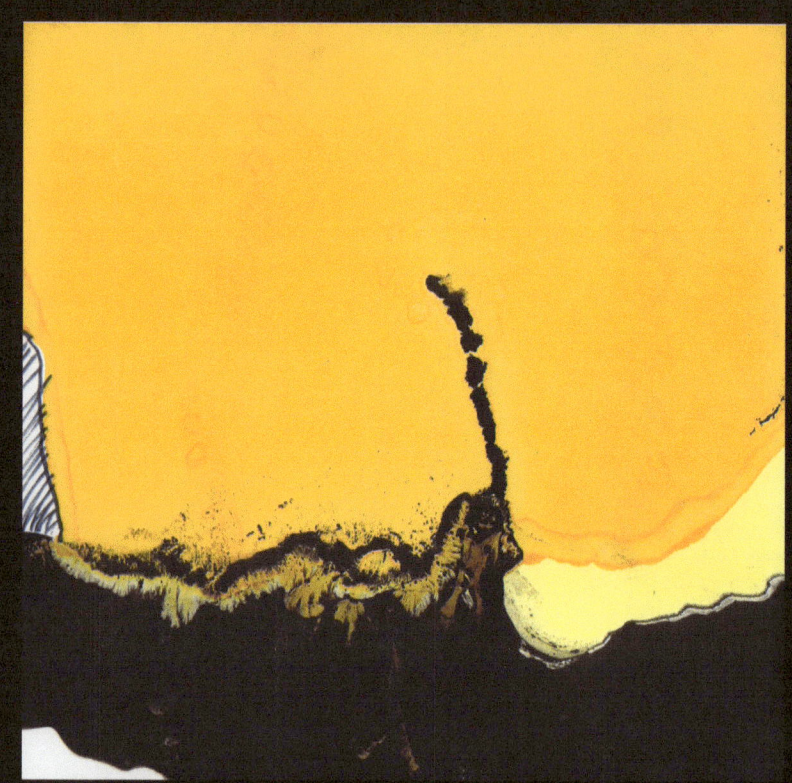

Shur
Salty, also name of one of the
Persian music modes, Dastgah Shur

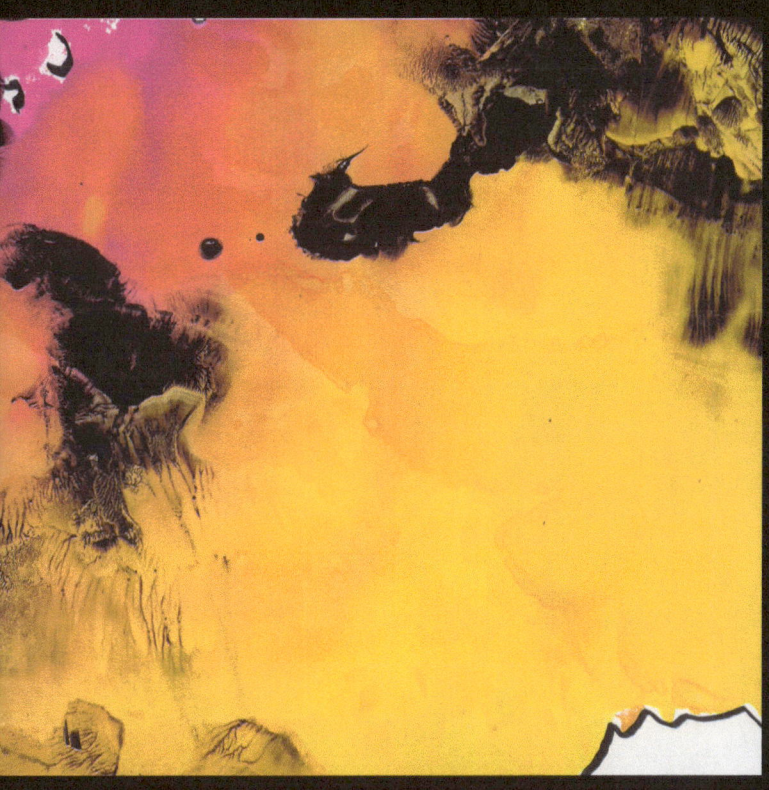

A'ama'al
Hope, wish

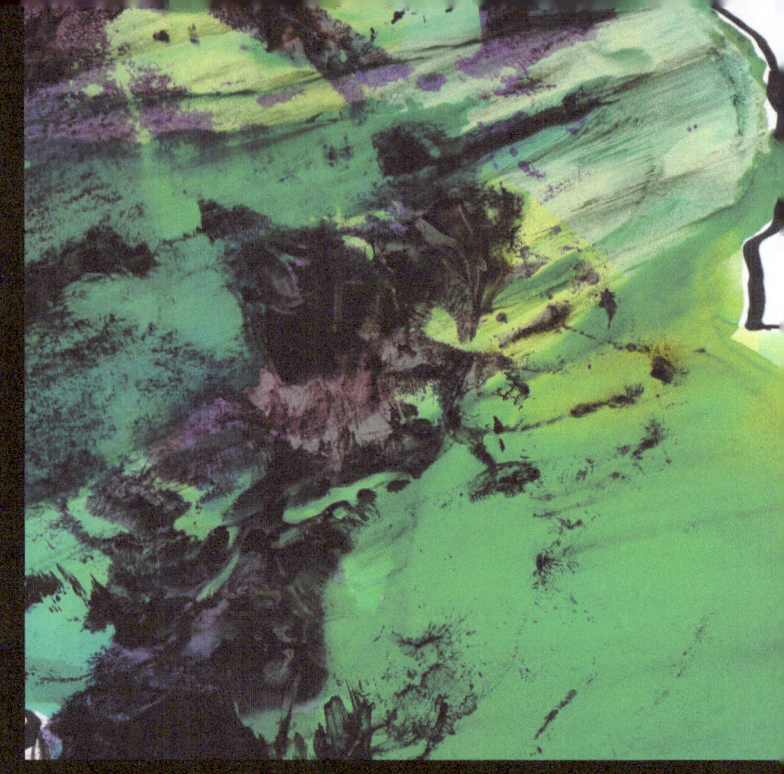

Bangar
Oath, commitment

3

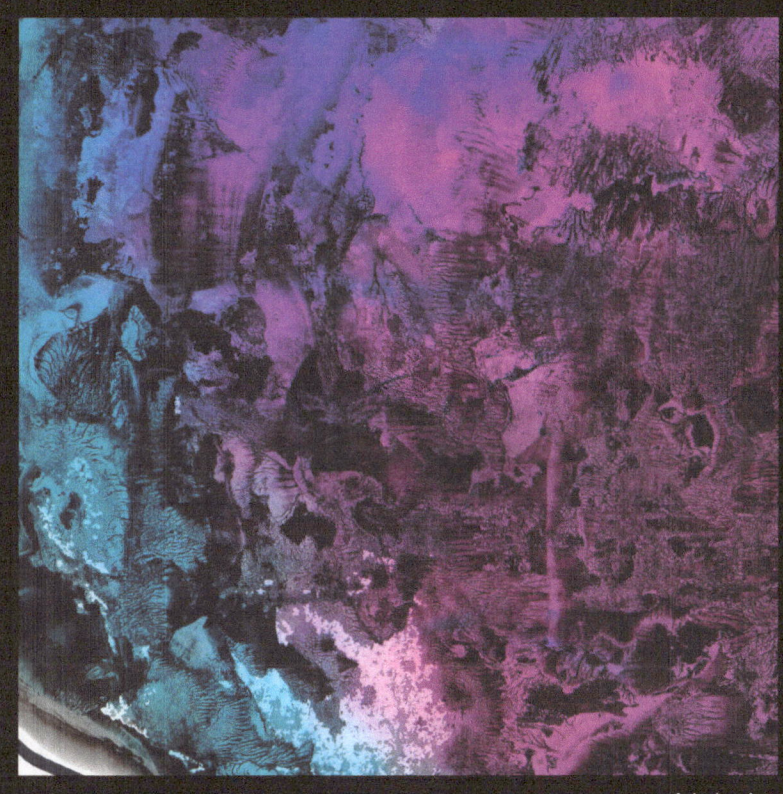

Naba'at
Depth of water

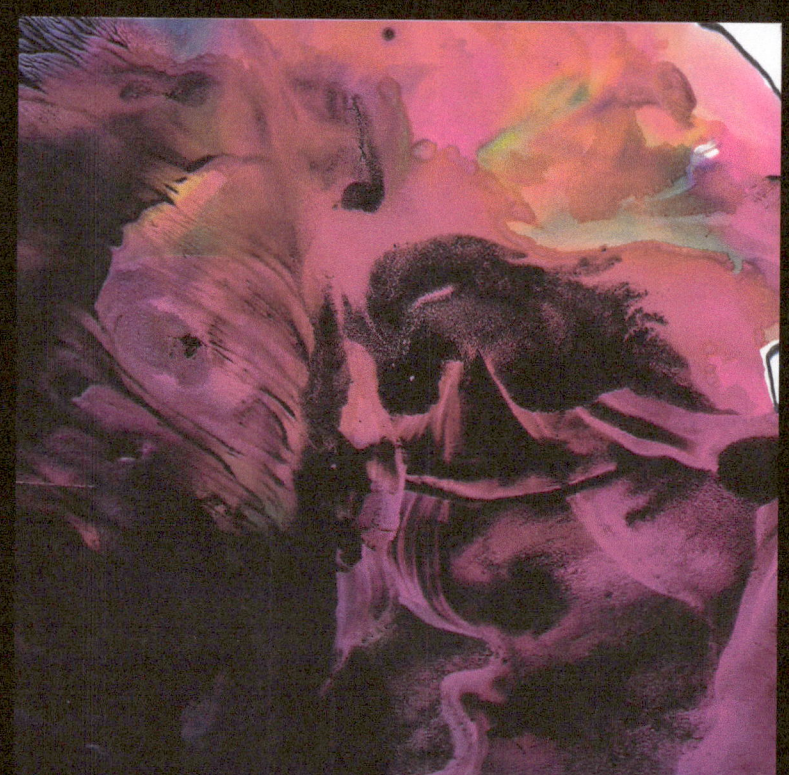

Fosoon
Magic

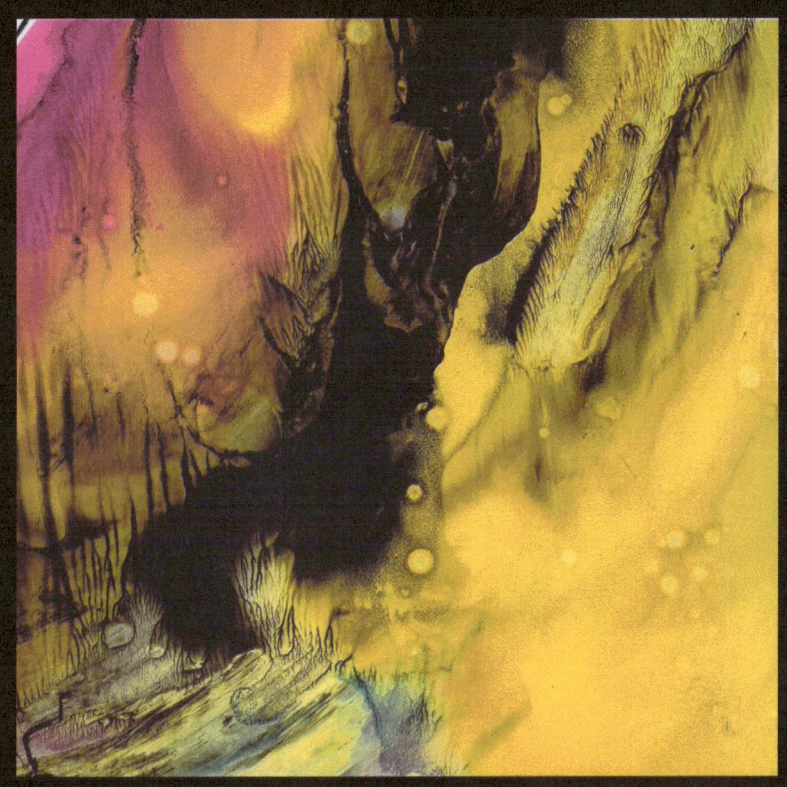

Ya'aba'an
Plain, desert

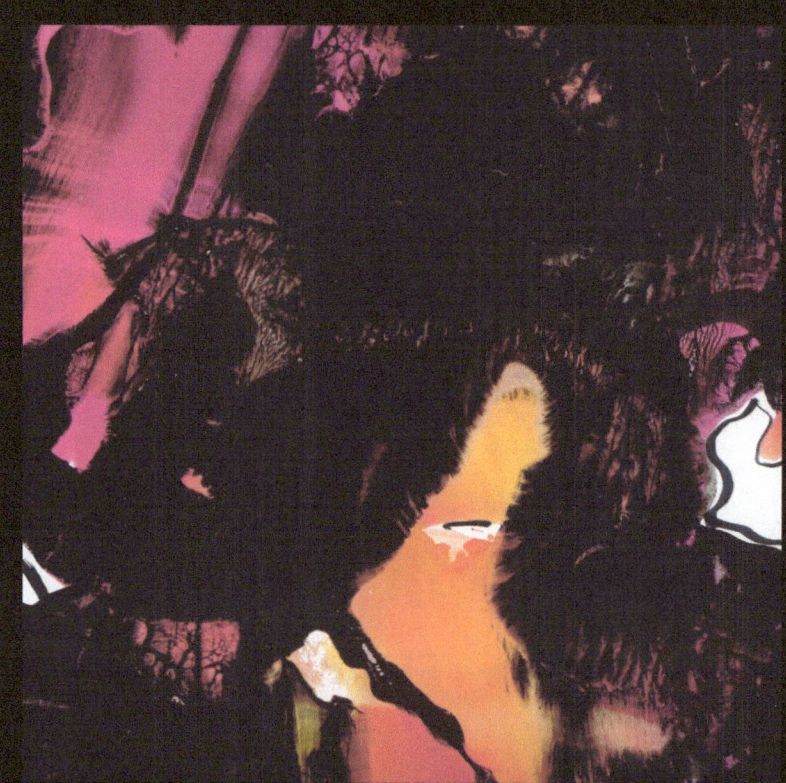

Makmoon
Covered, hidden

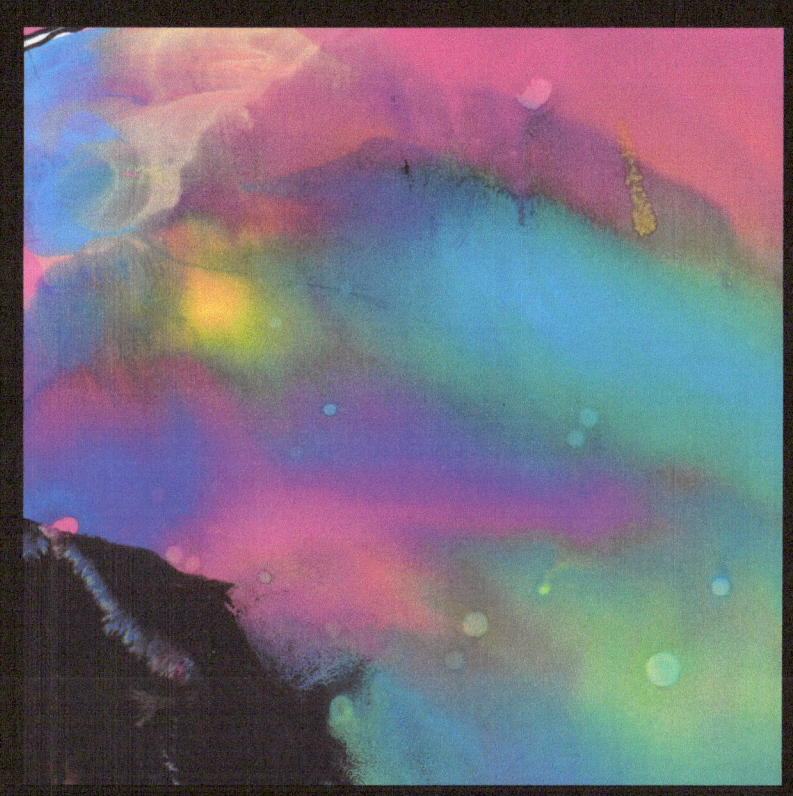

Ra'ah
Joy, happiness

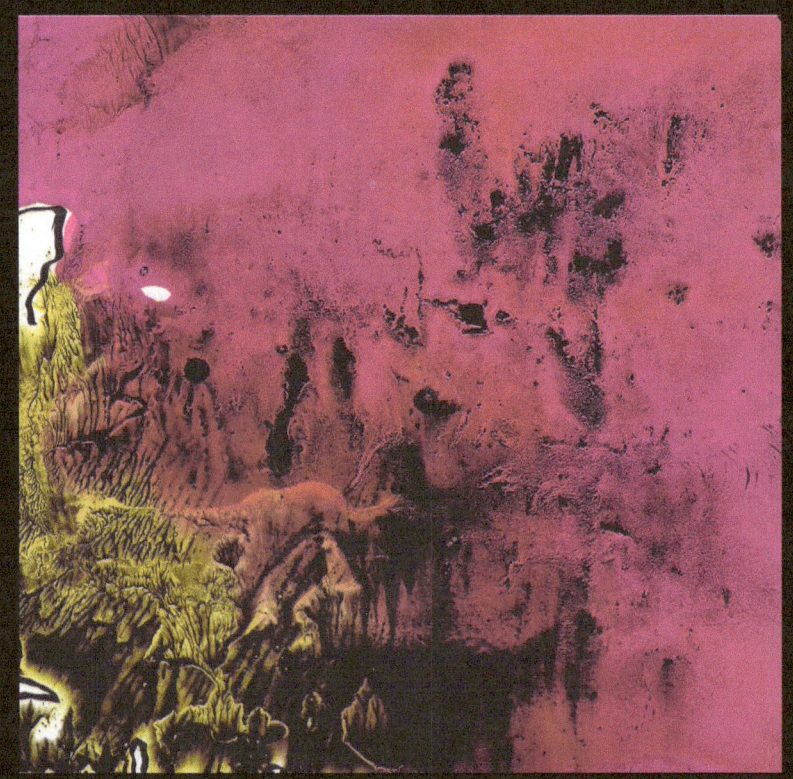

Araz
Clear

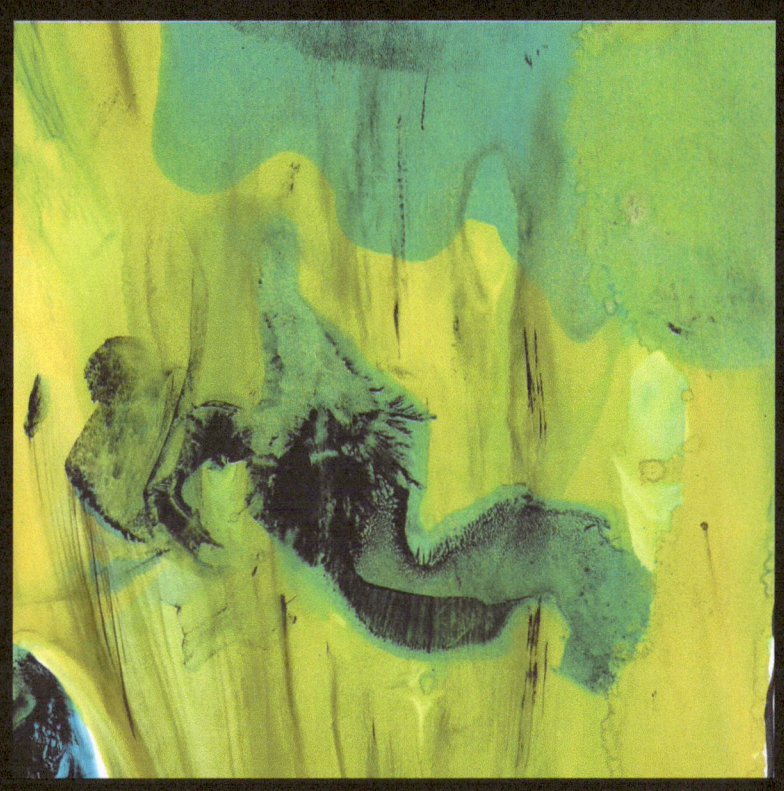

Kera'al
A fertile land

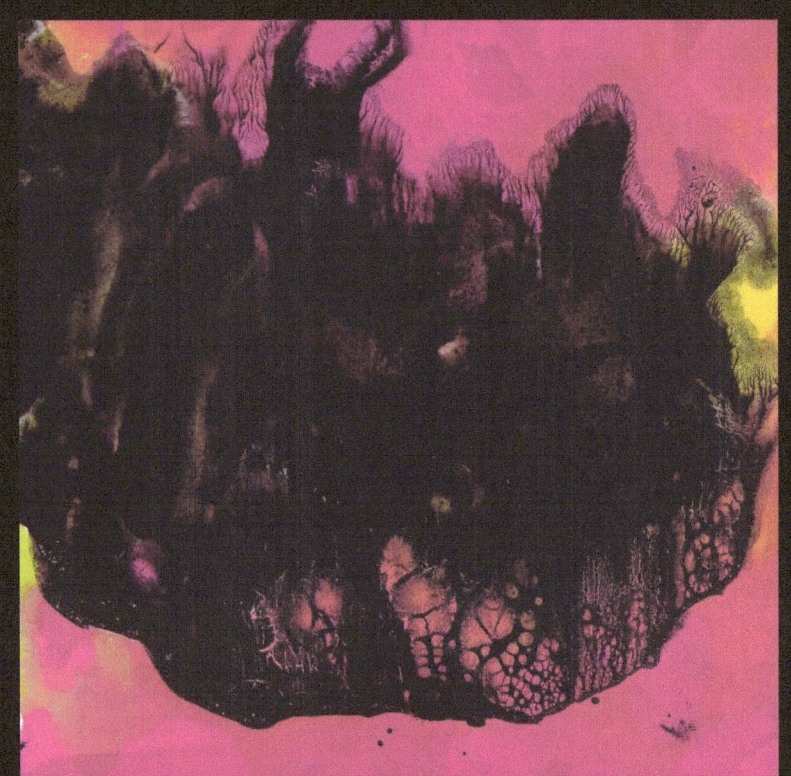

Yalma'a
Any large and light object

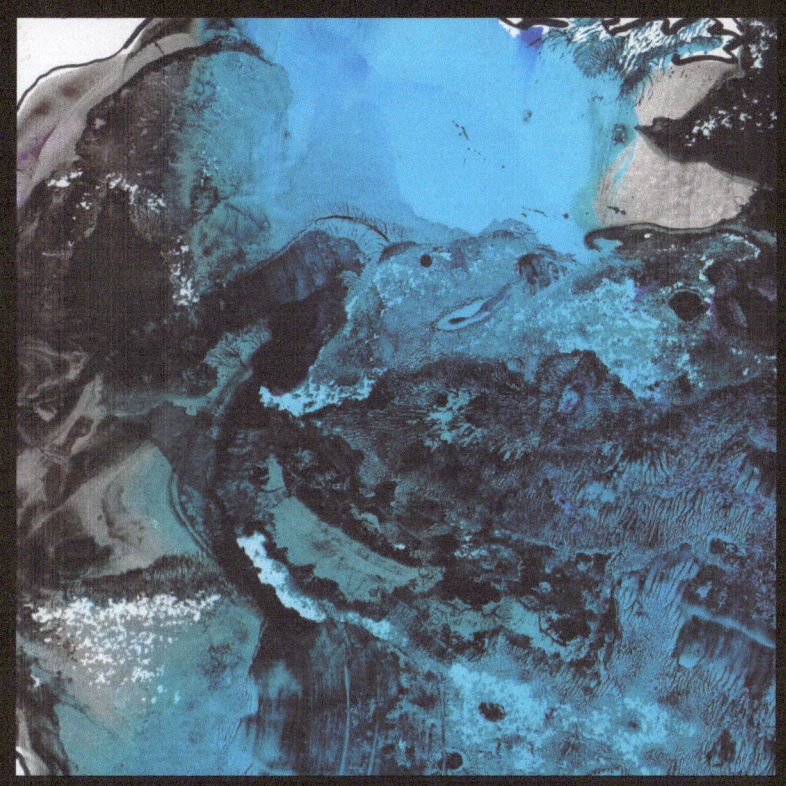

Sa'ayan
To grind, a combination of blue and green

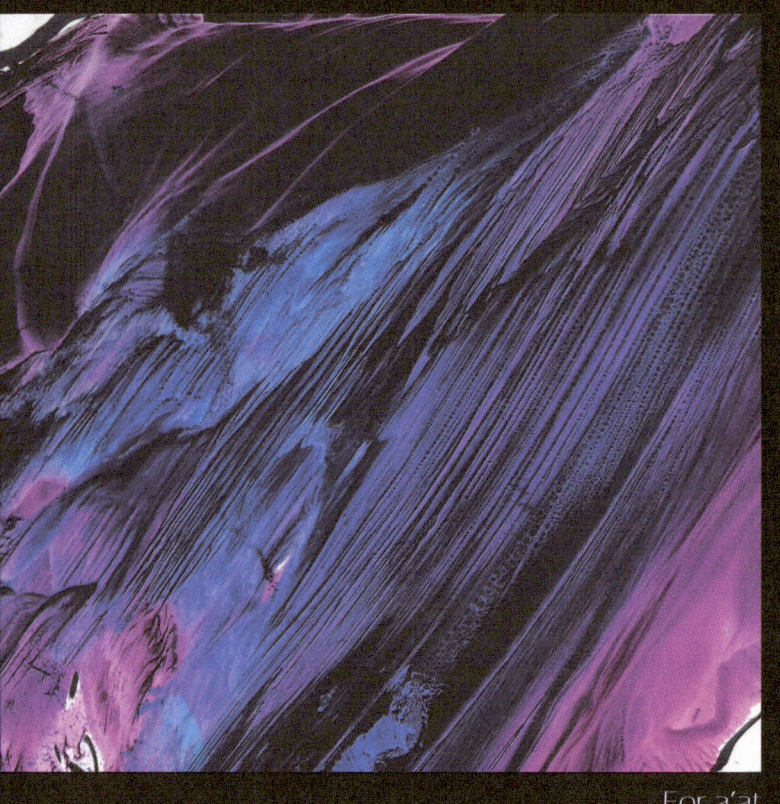

For a'at
Non-saline water

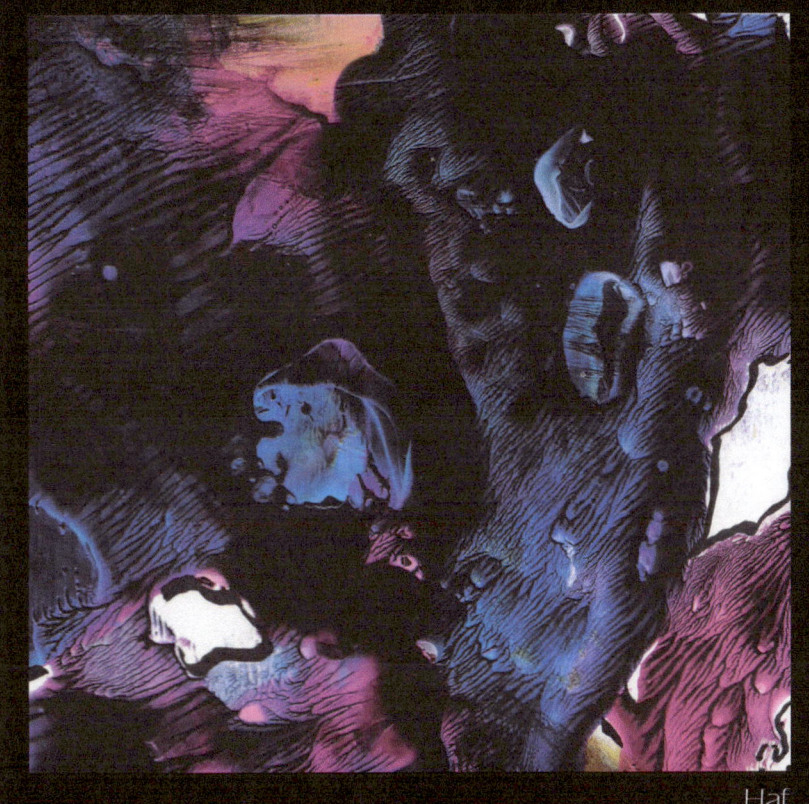

Haf
Stopped rain

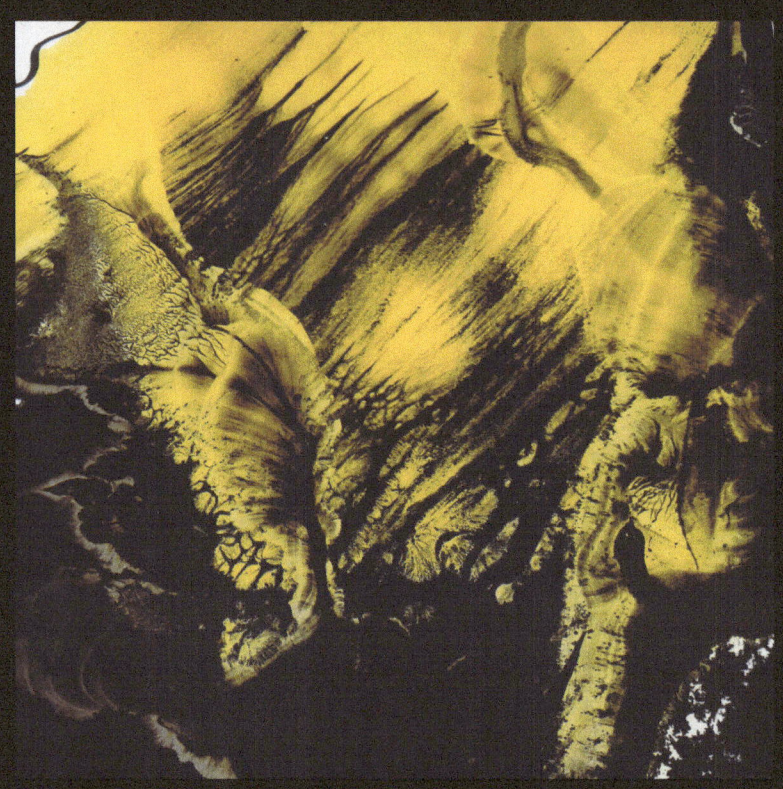

Da'araj
Exhilarated, booster

15

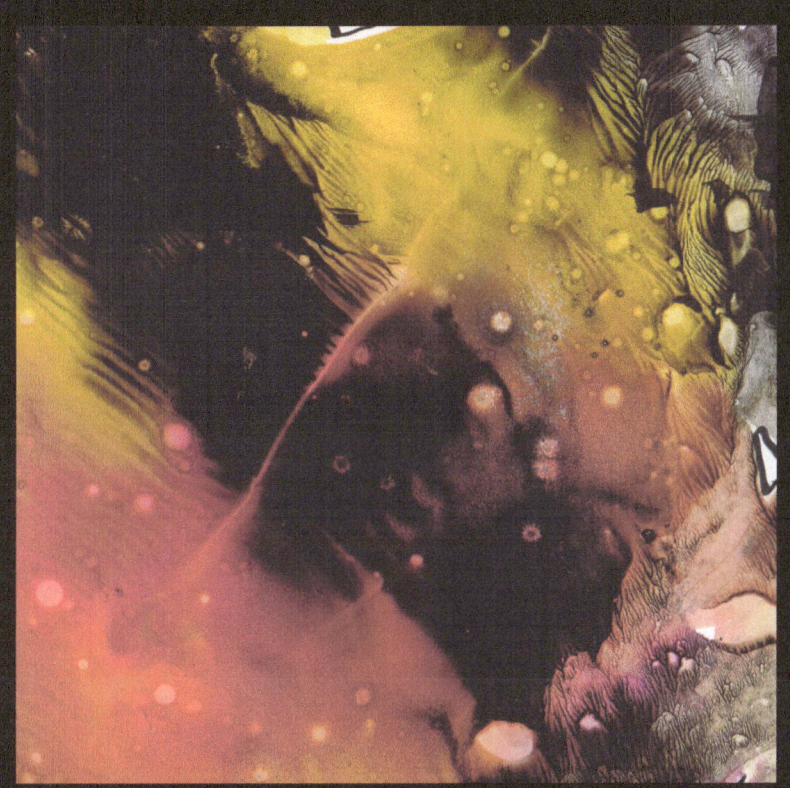

Baqr
Cleaving

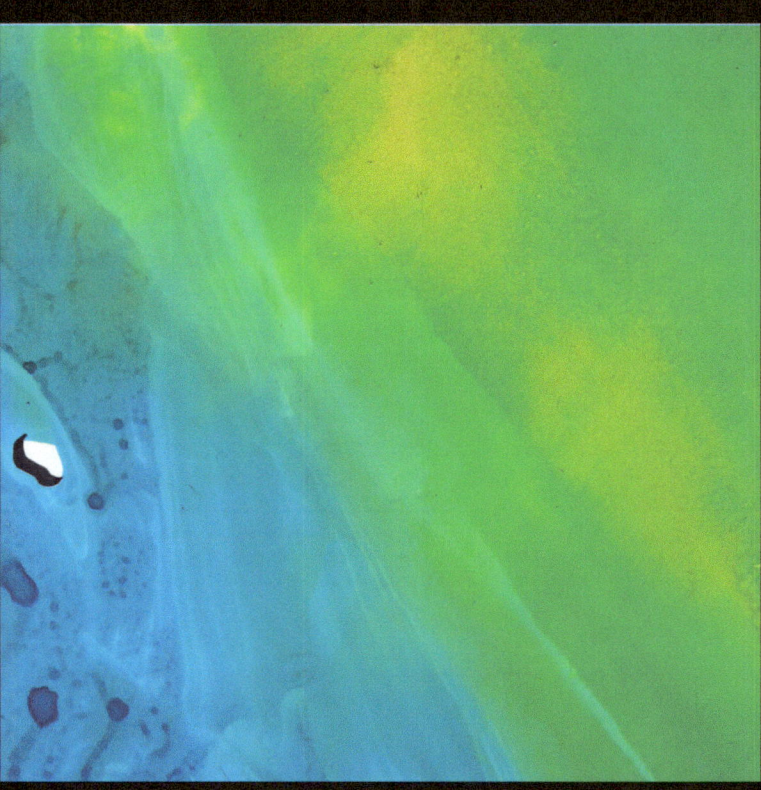

Tima'a
Plain

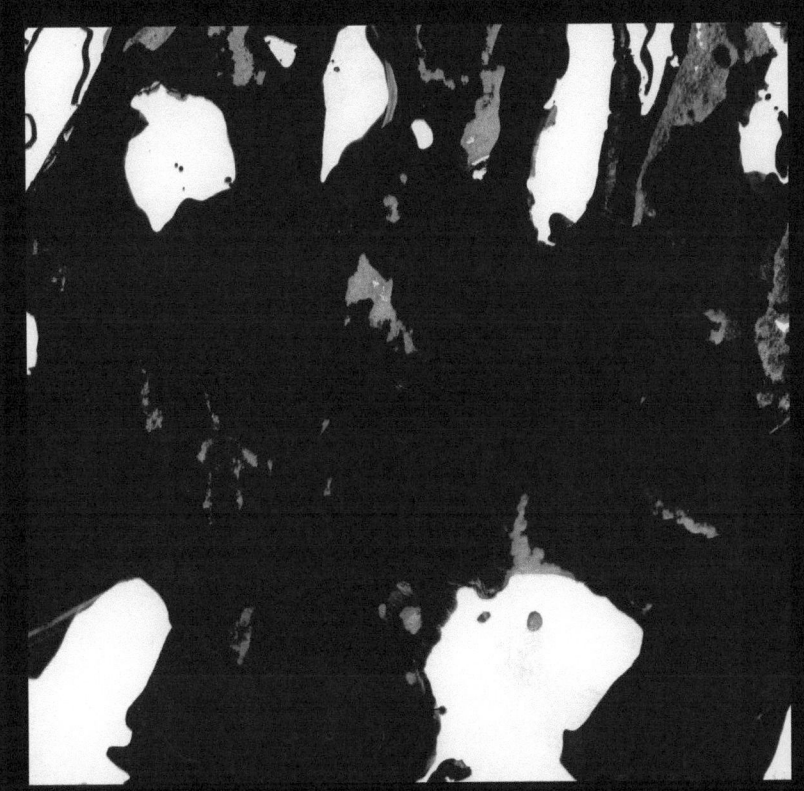

A'asel
Original

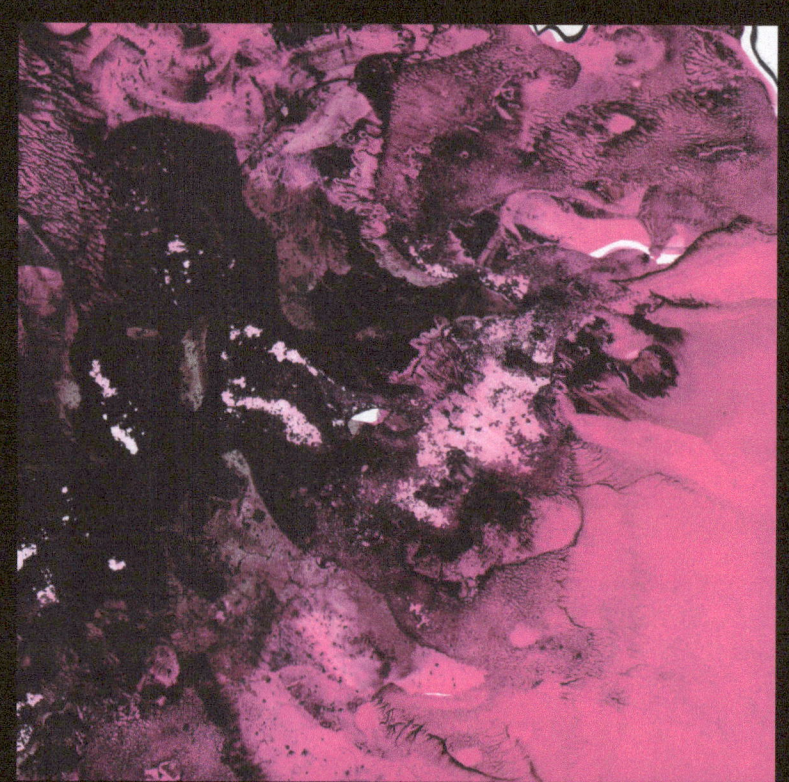

Vasna'a
Full

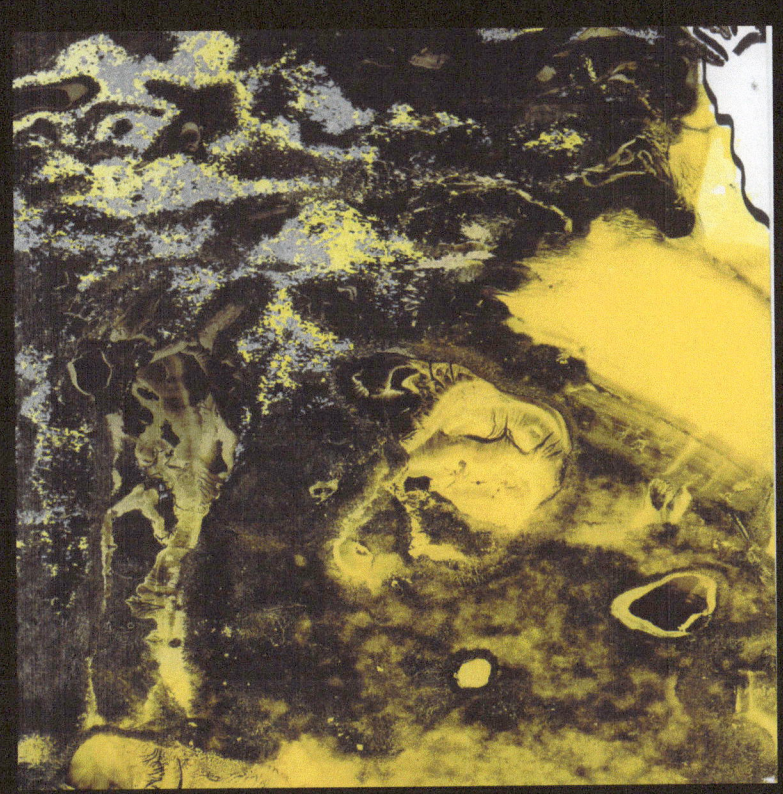

Sha'azaneh
A fragile golden-black stone

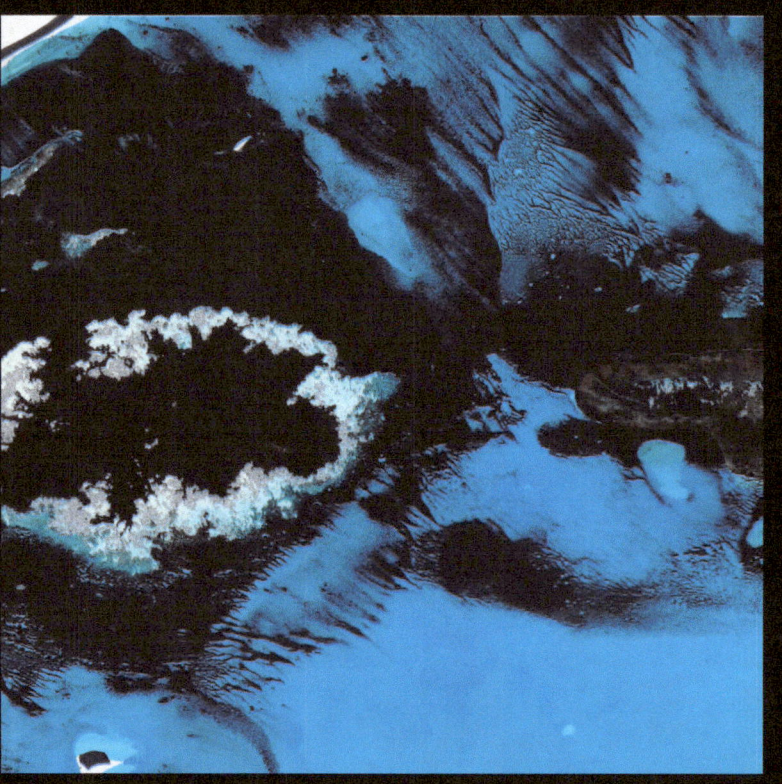

Ya'ad
Remembrance, memory

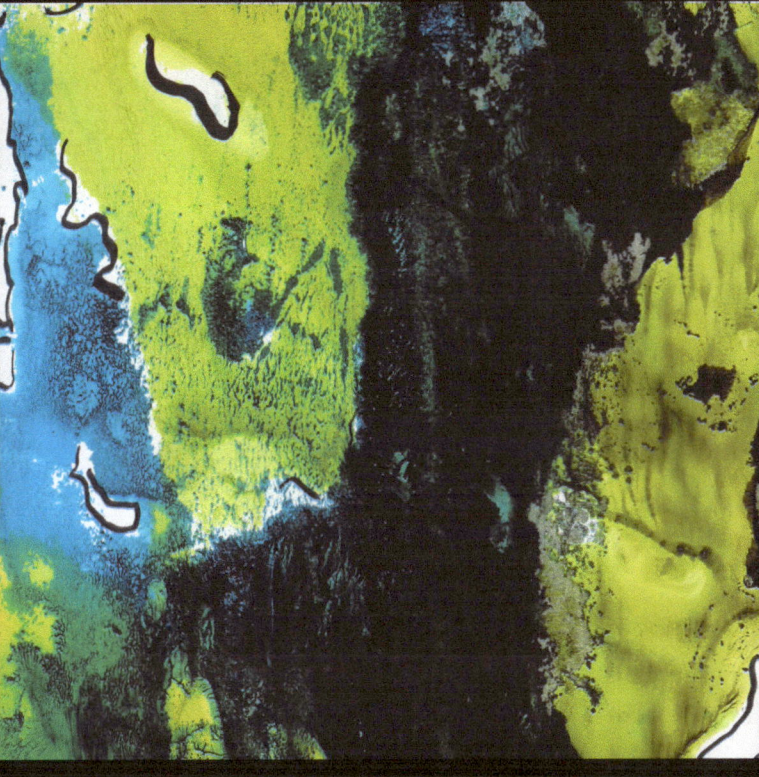

Ra'az
Indian word, to describe the earth

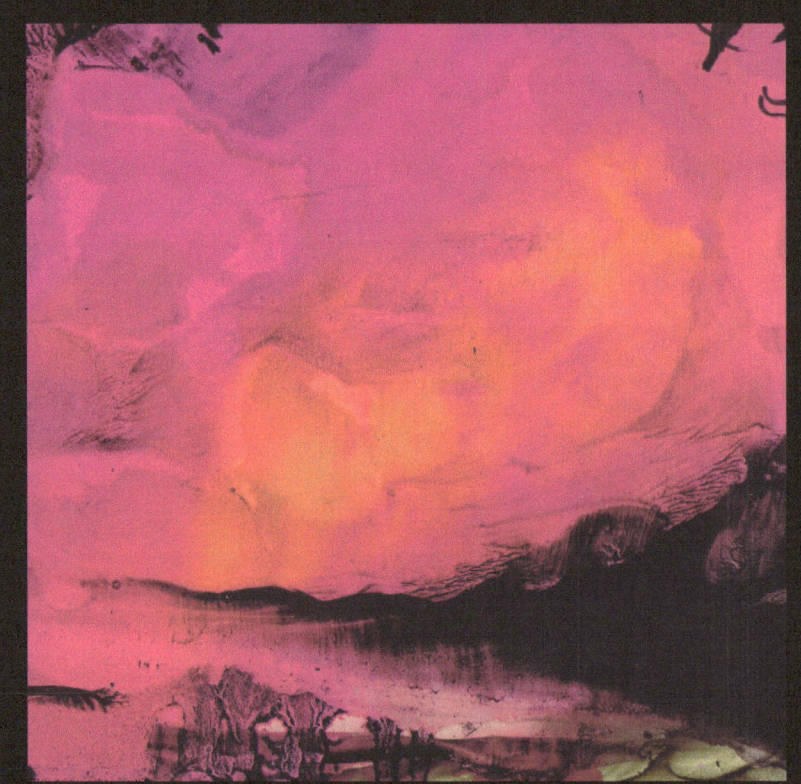

Masa'a
Sunset, nightfall

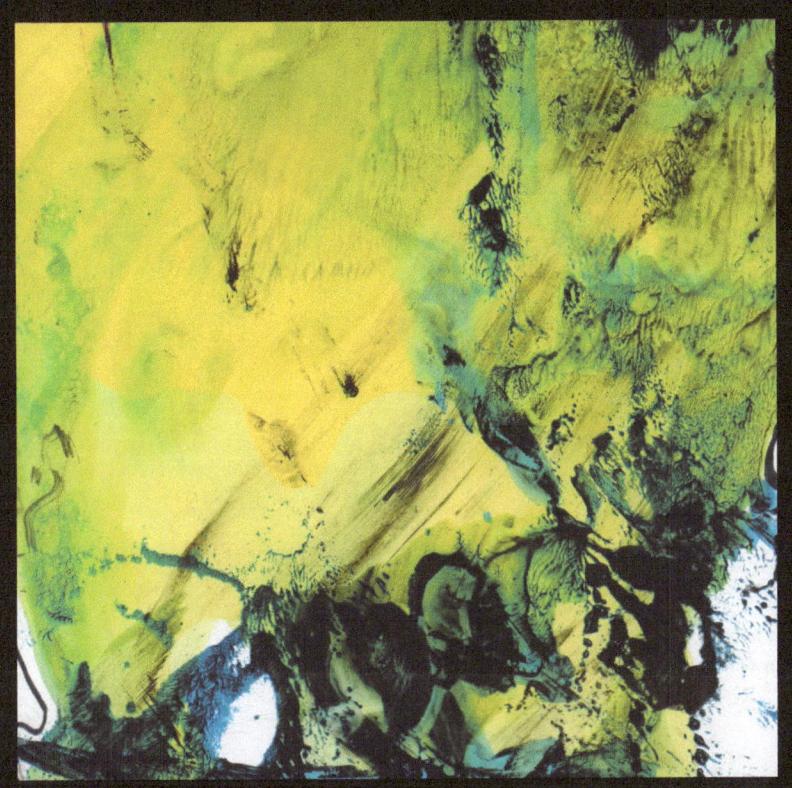

Fa'adaj
A yellowish-greenish white stone
showing other colors as well

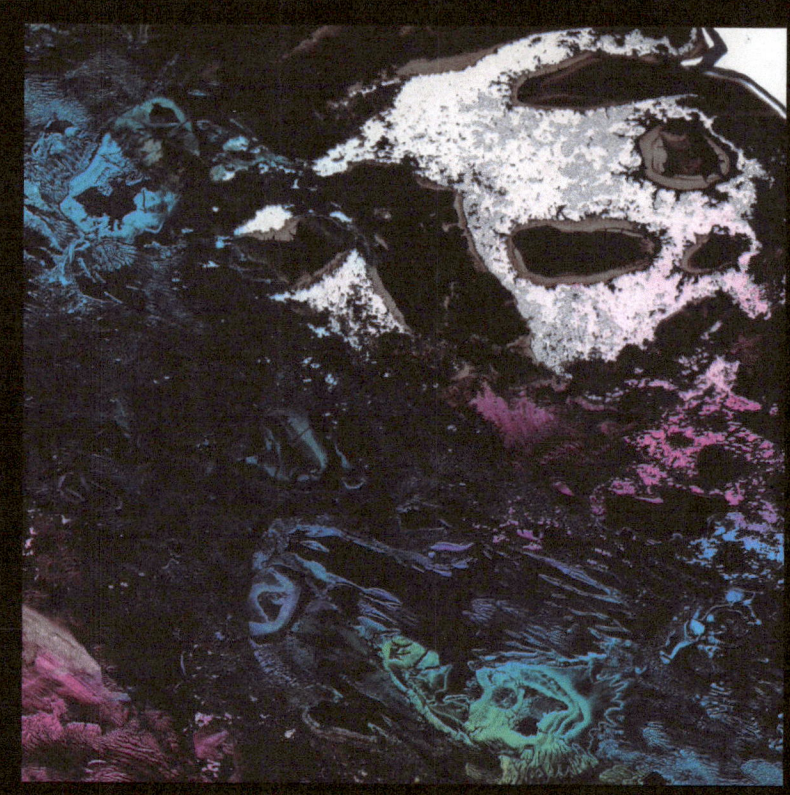

Cha'ama'aheh
Indian word, a day to welcome the moon

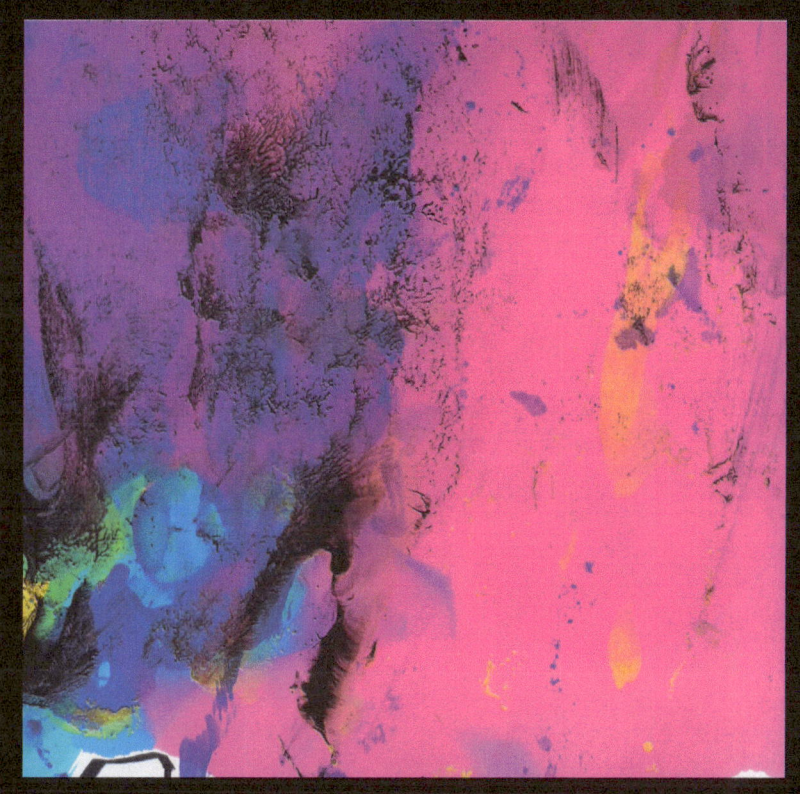

Ra'ad
A hardworking, generous person

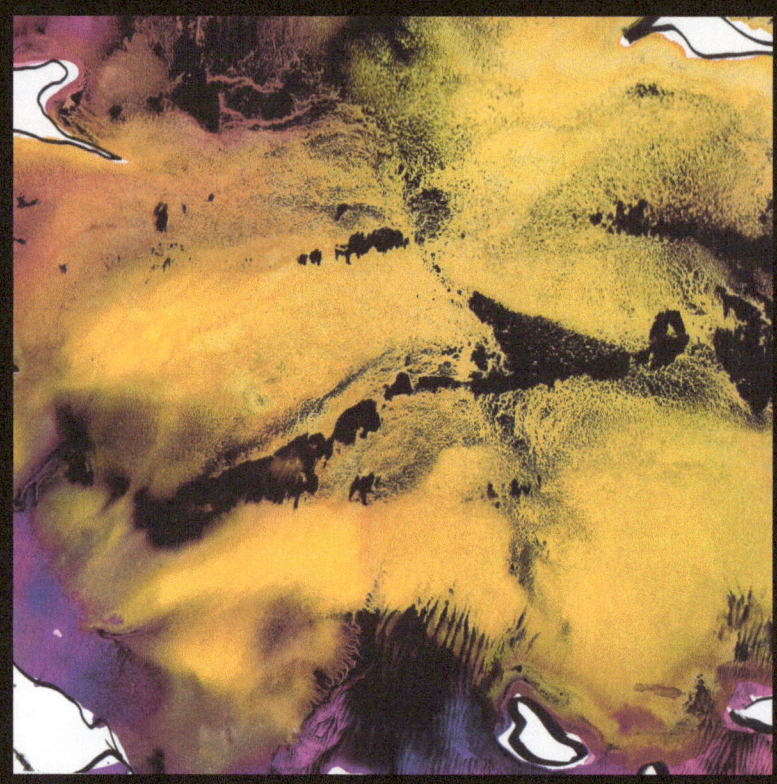

Bosraq
Yellow ruby

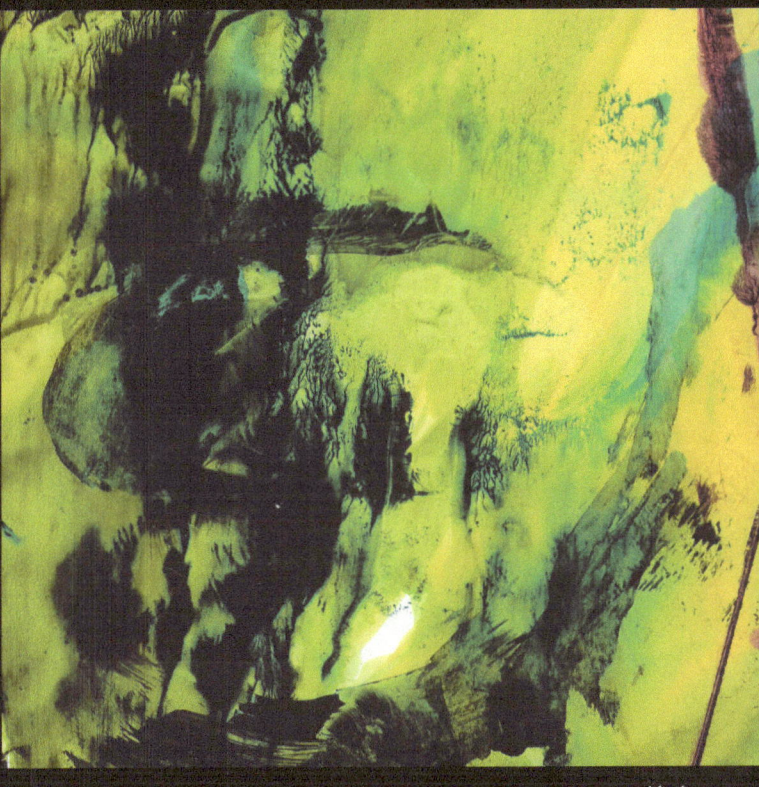

Ka'atoozi
Devout

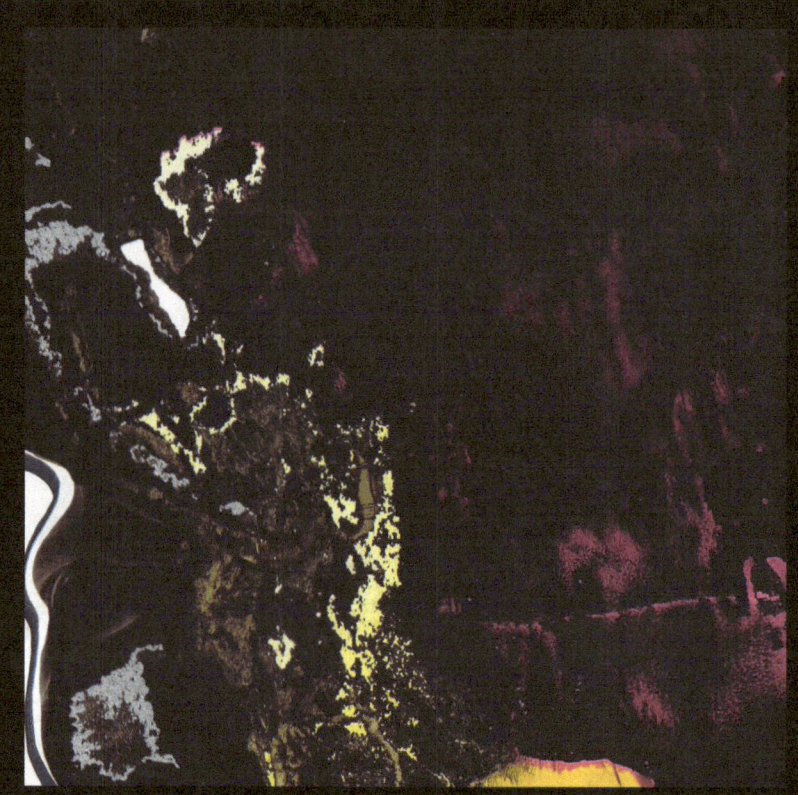

Da'ash
A furnace

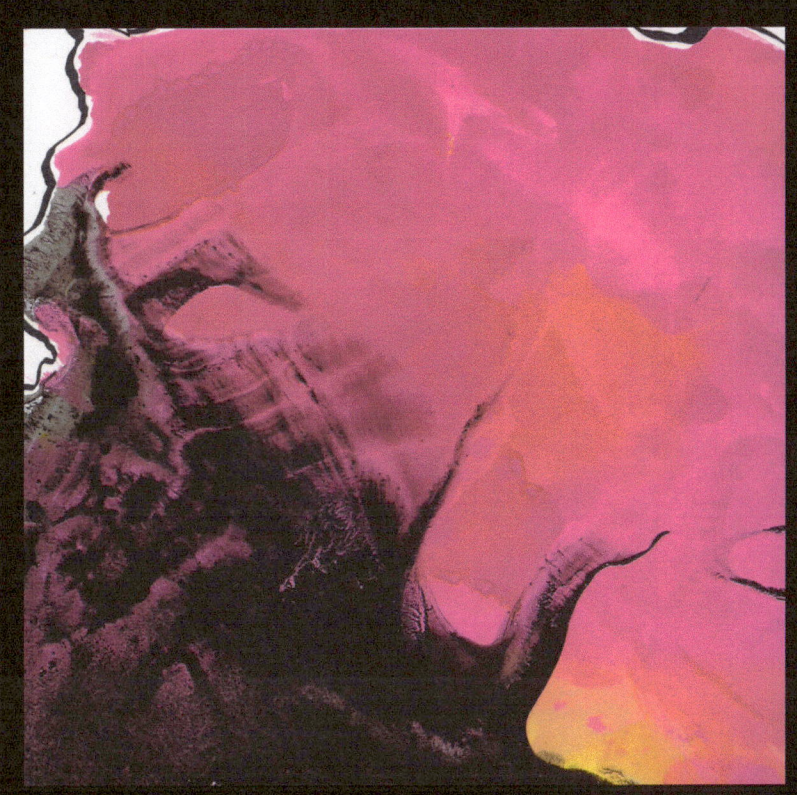

Ta'az
Beloved

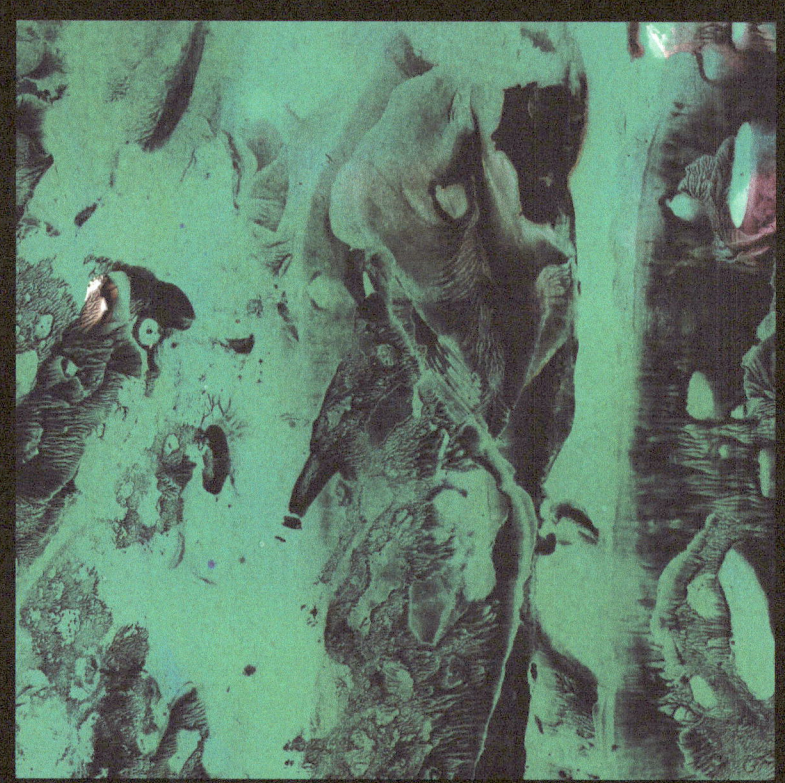

Na'arvan
A shadowy tree with lots of leaves

31

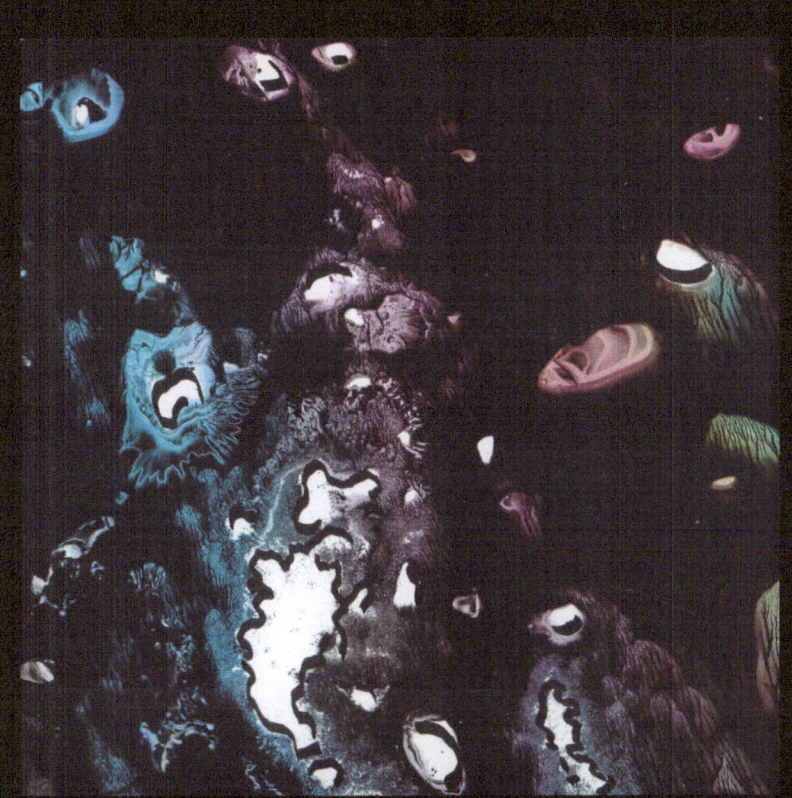

Santez
Combination of elements

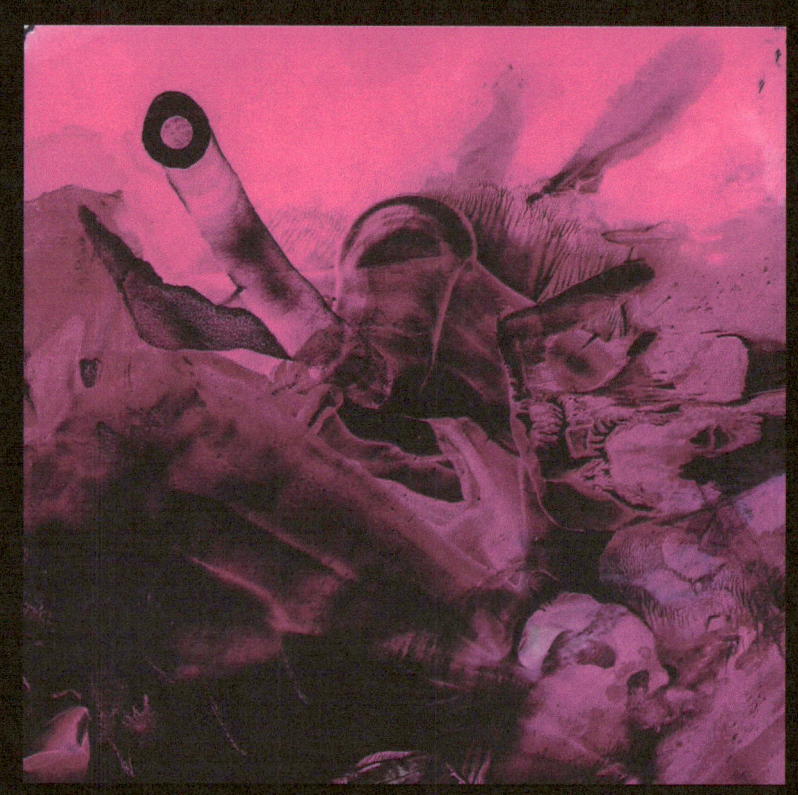

Ato
Colorful, pink

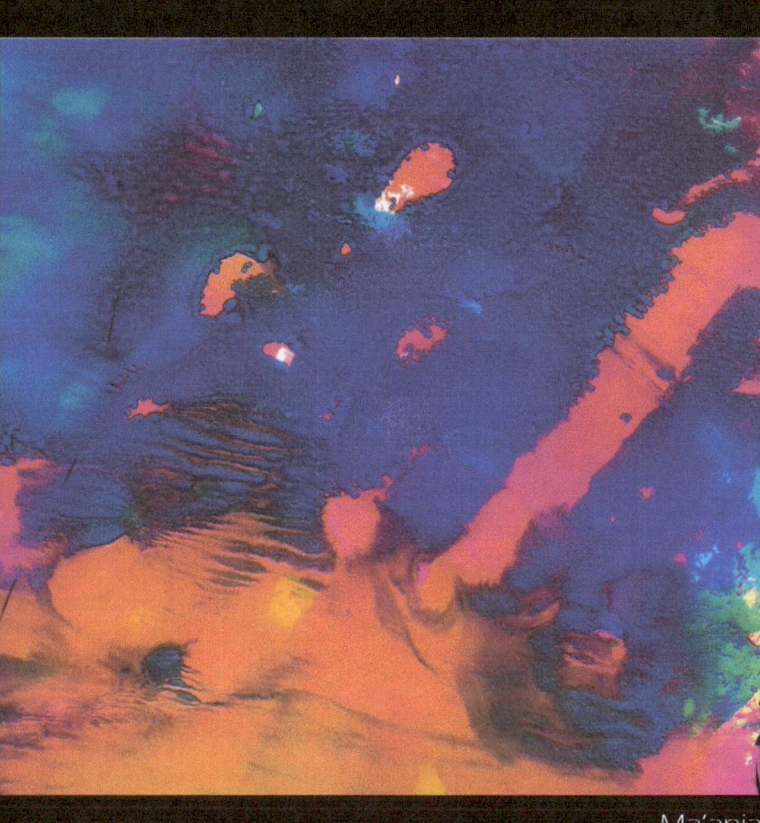

Ma'ania
Mania, of predators

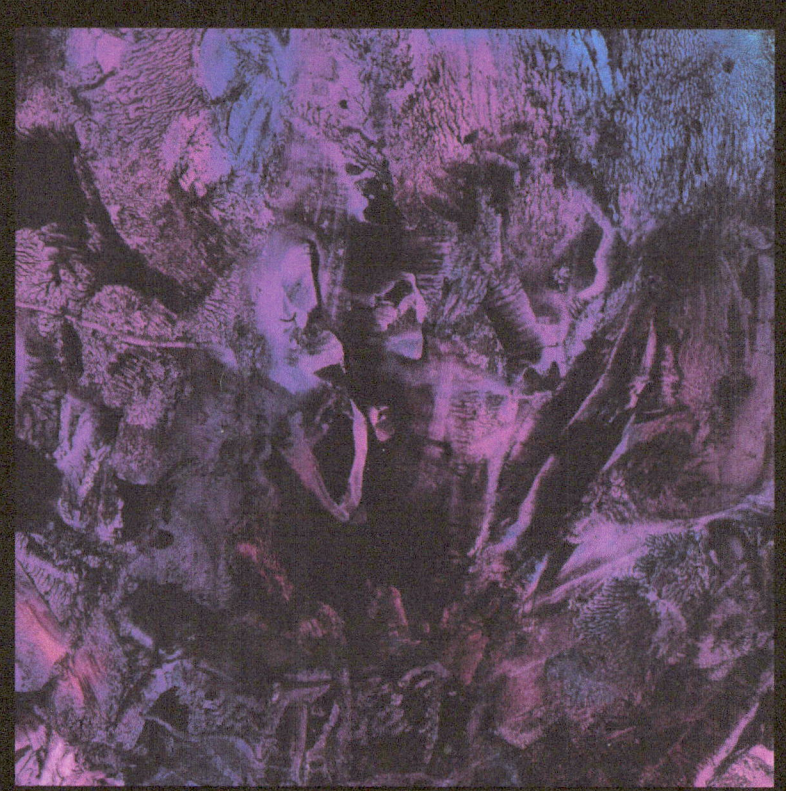

La'ai
Mud

35

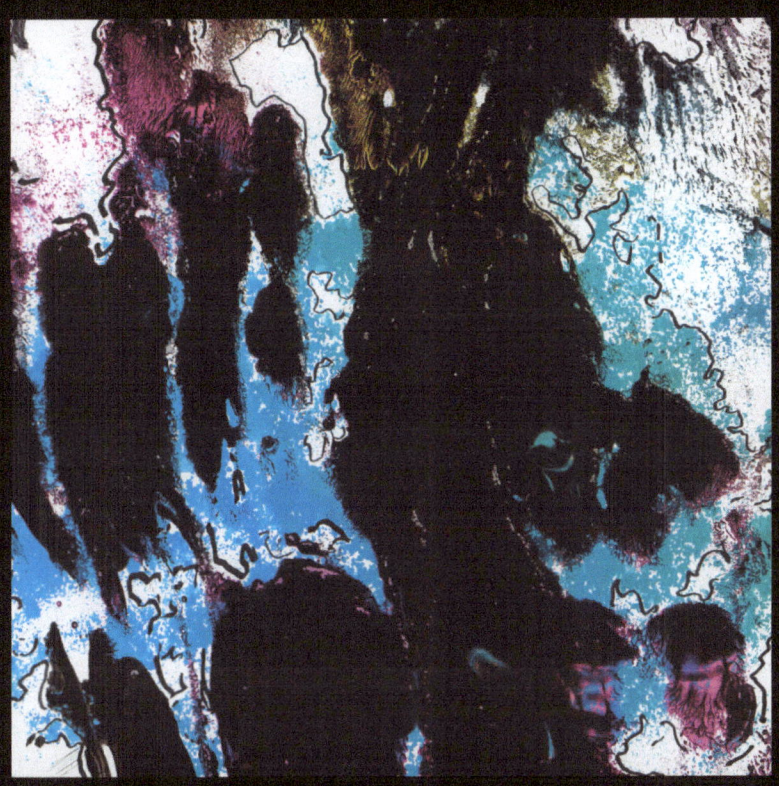

Fa'ahem
Black, still water

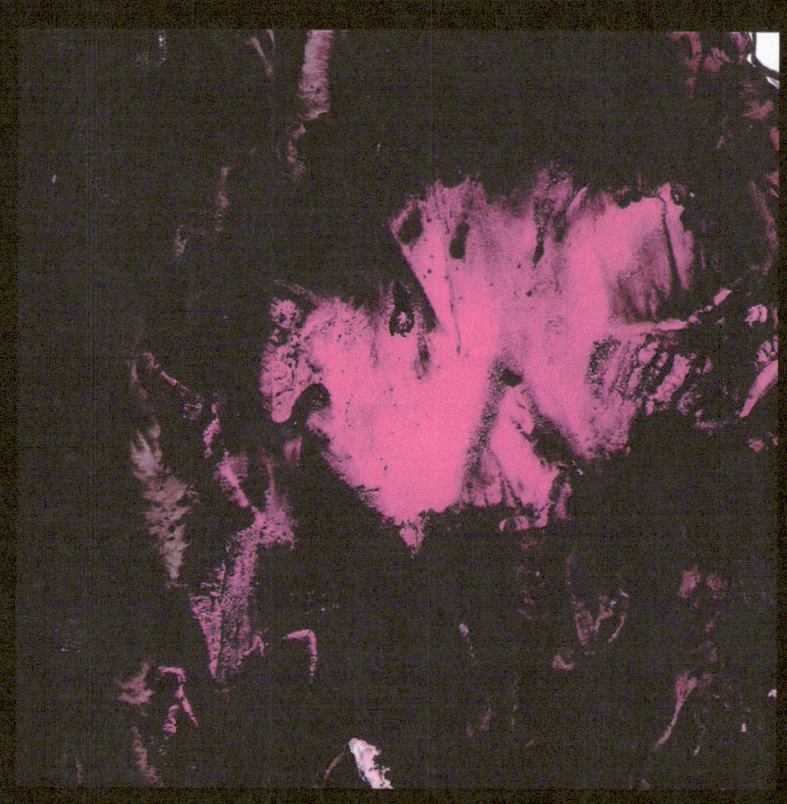

Pegasus
Constellation, a winged horse

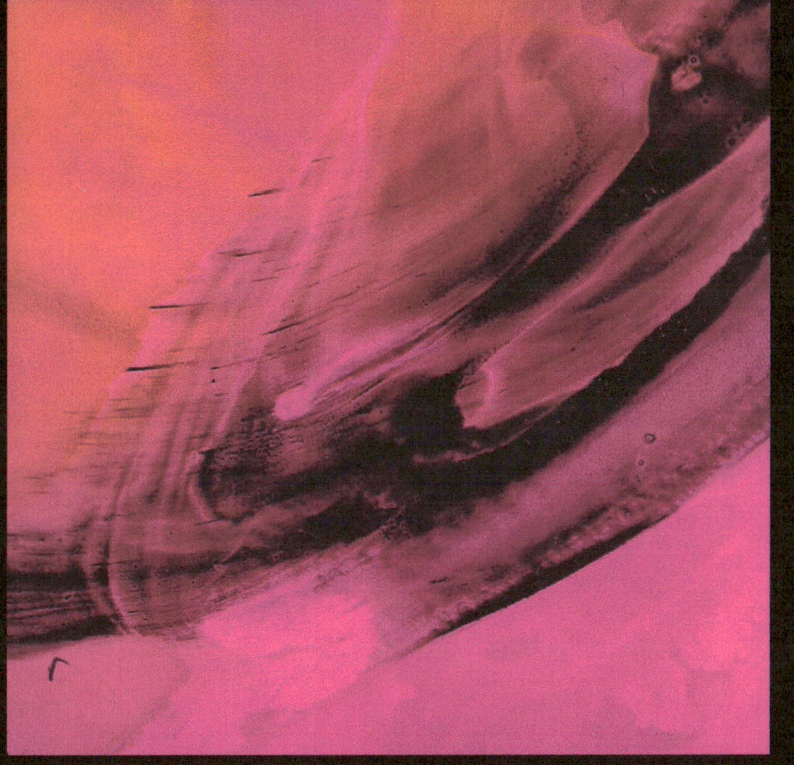

Chang

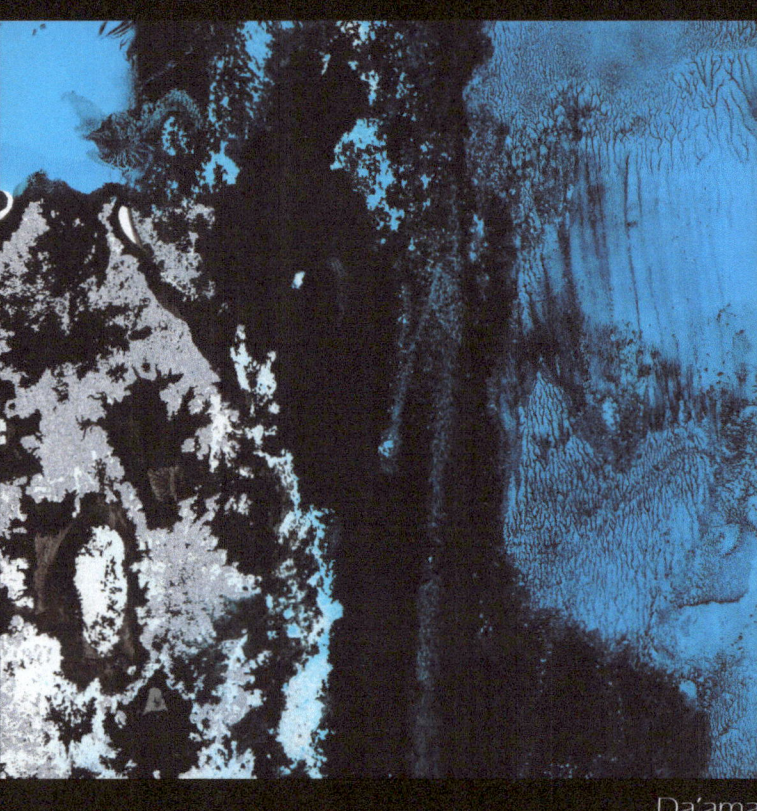

Da'ama
Sea

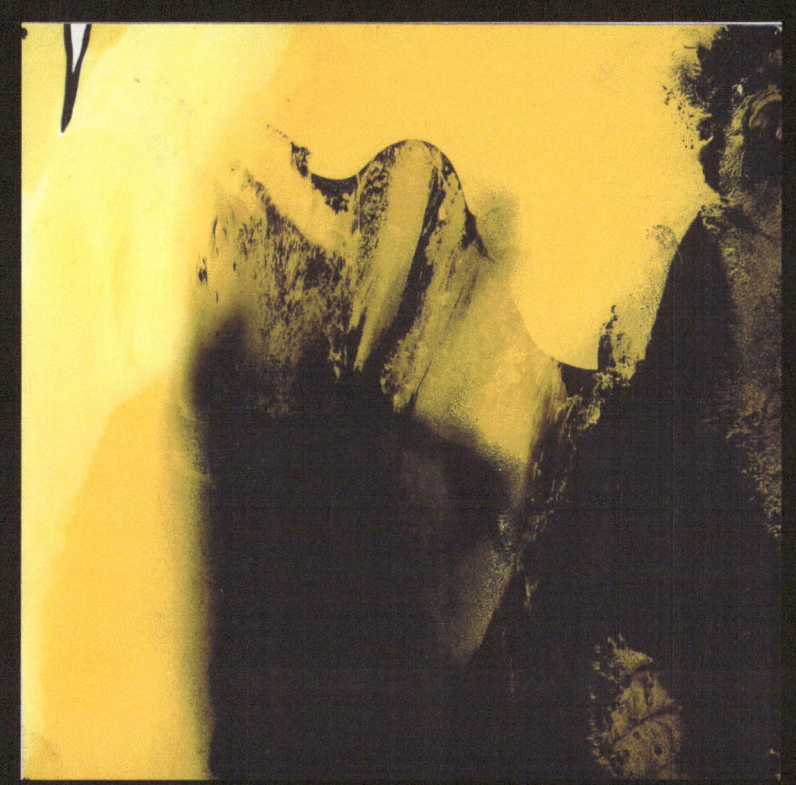

Shak
Doubt

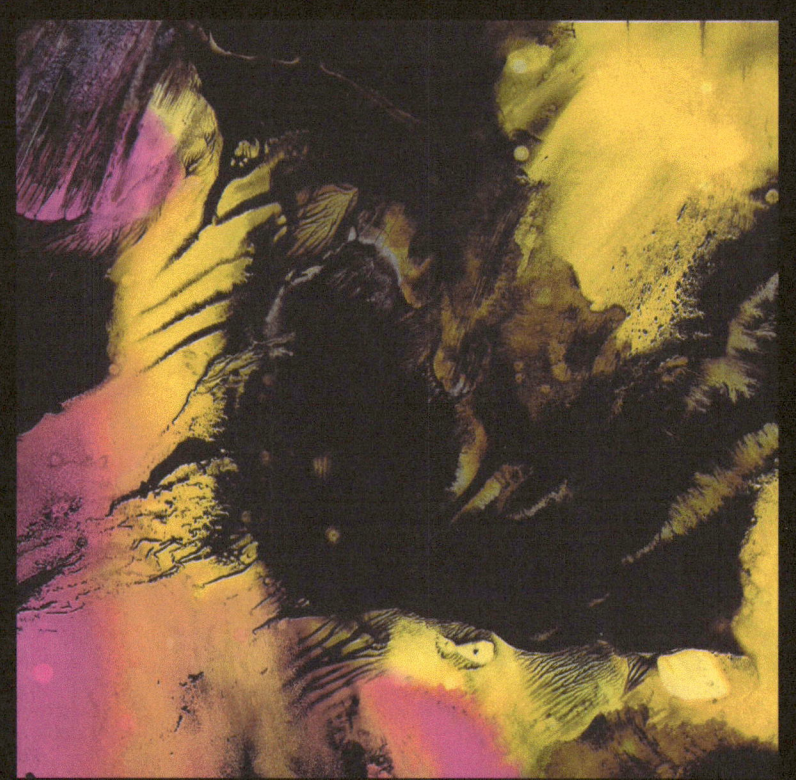

Vaqd

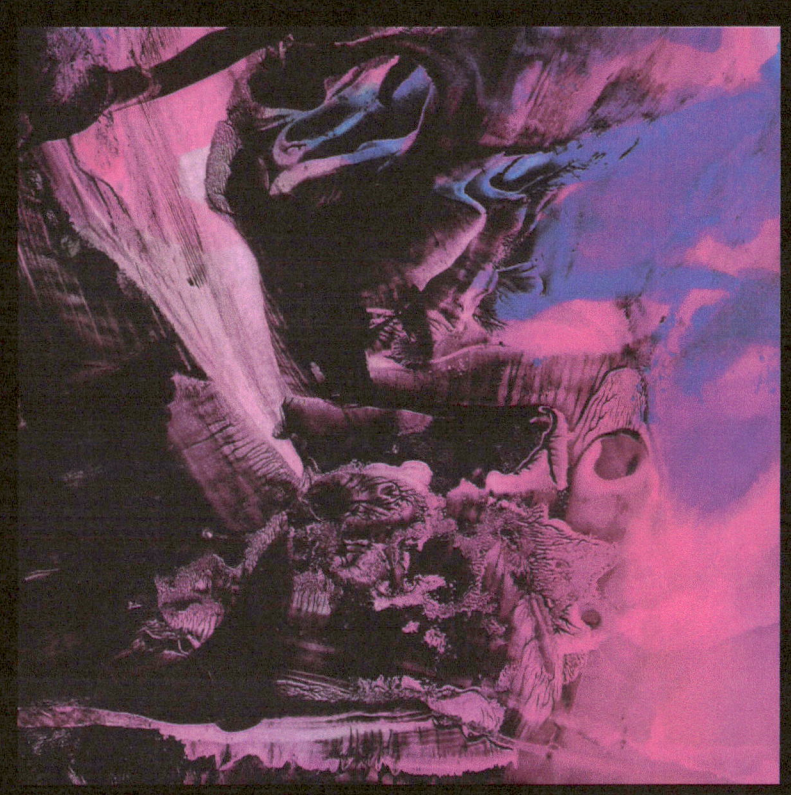

Delta
Delta, a piece of land shaped like
a triangle formed when a river splits into
smaller rivers before it flows into an ocean

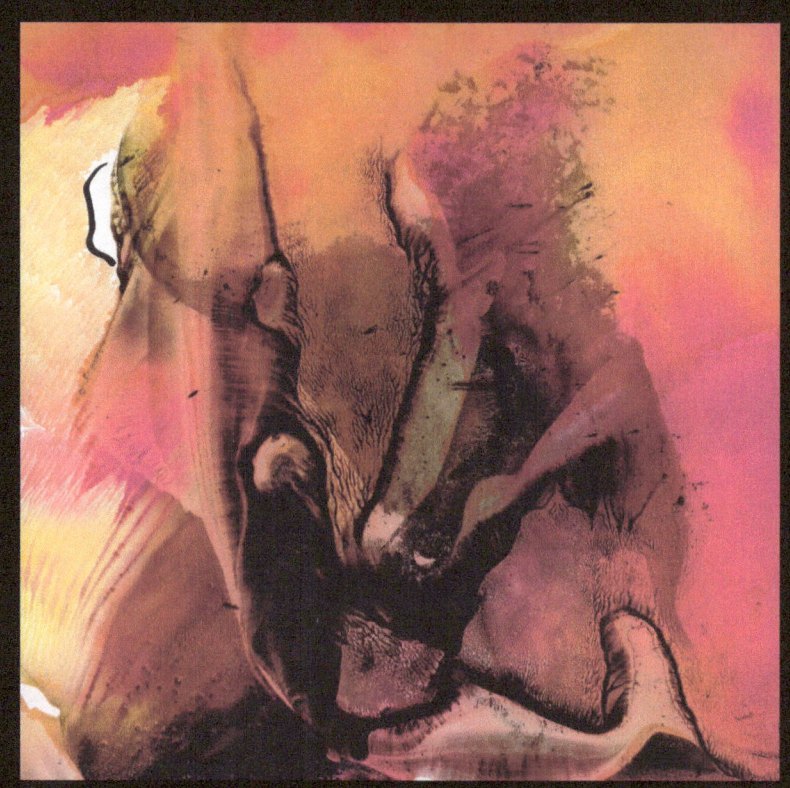

Karbal
A plant with bright, shiny, red flowers

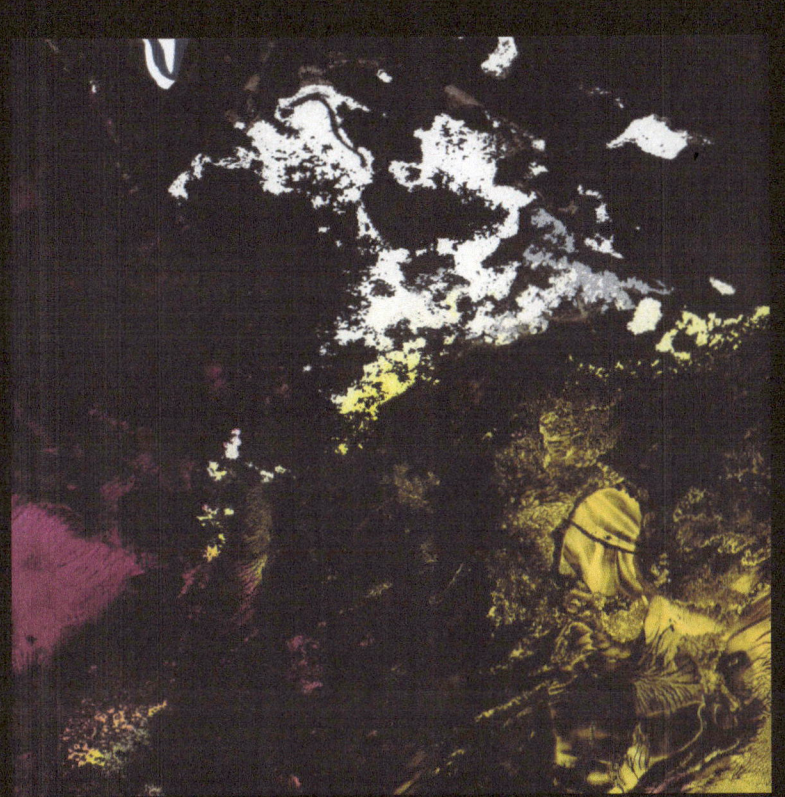

Banas
Escaping from evil

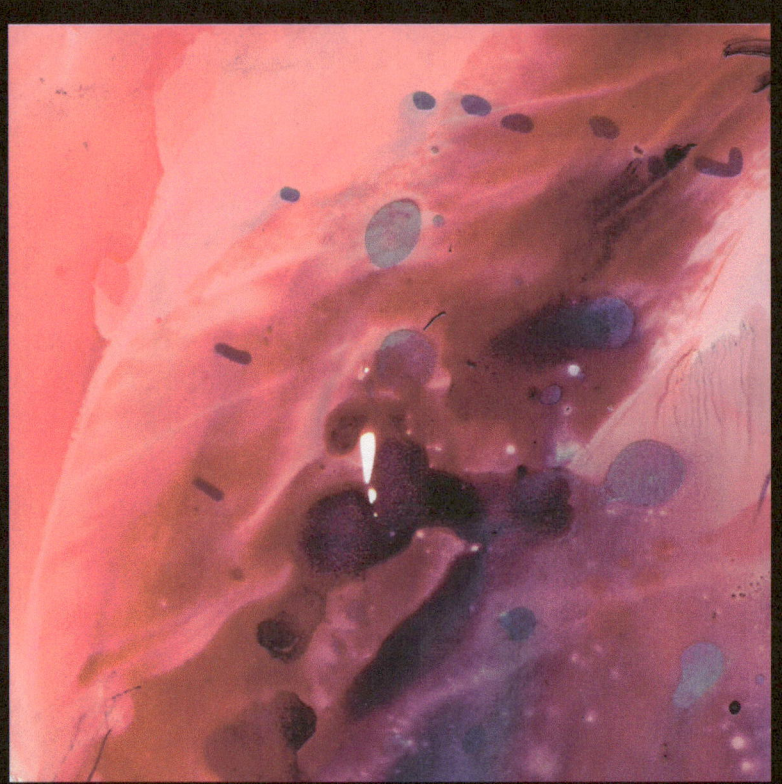

A'ali
Light red

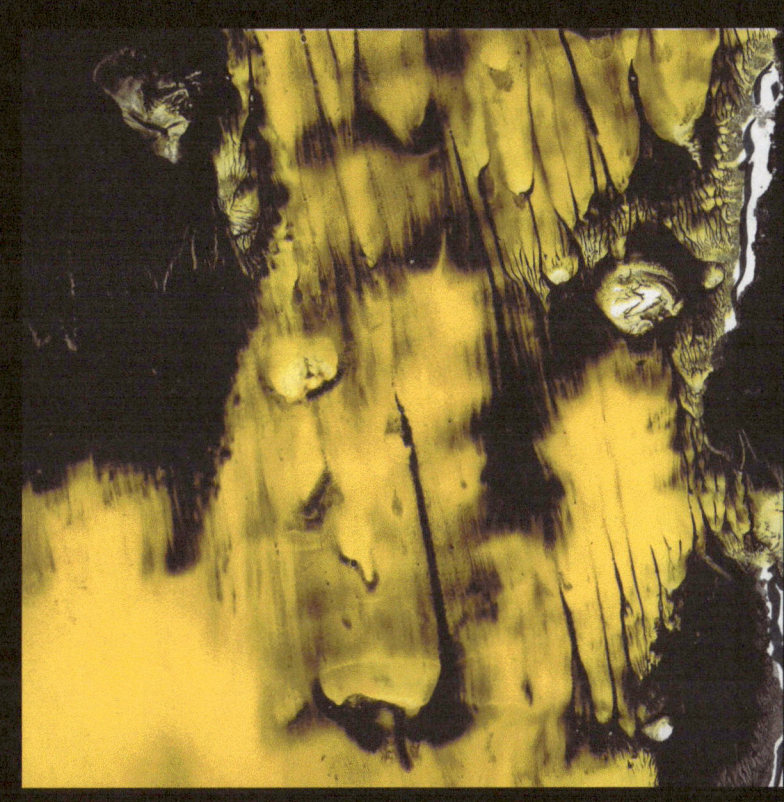

Ta'abak
Worry, having fever

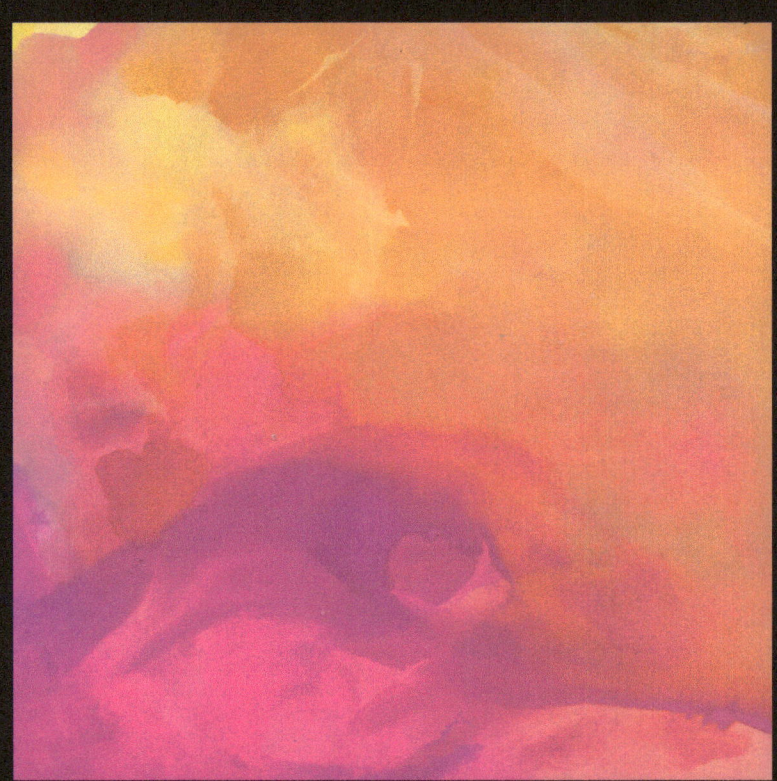

Madkh
Glory

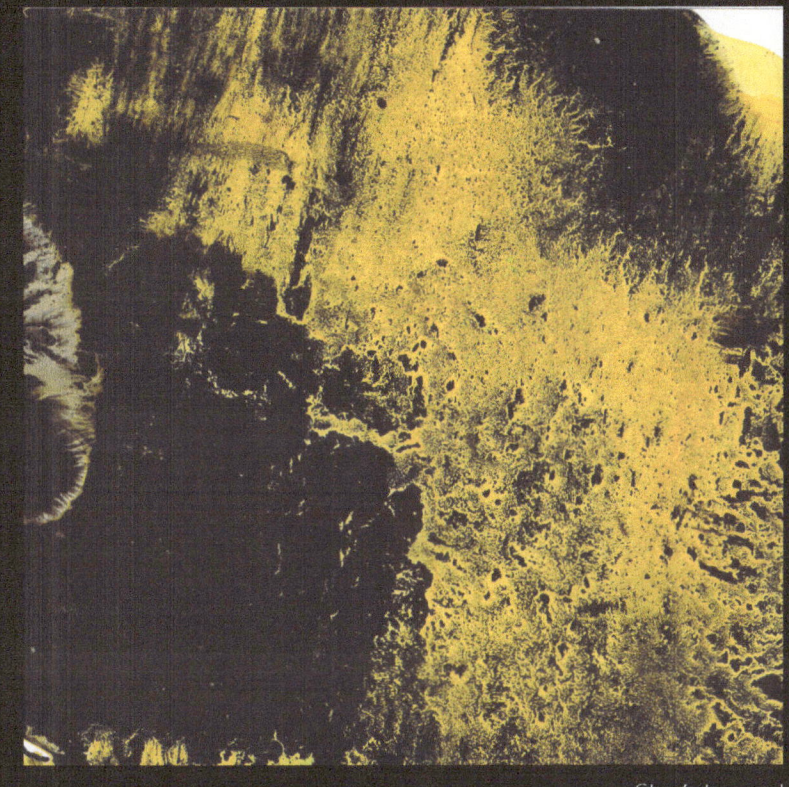

Sha'aboord
Halo, moon harvest

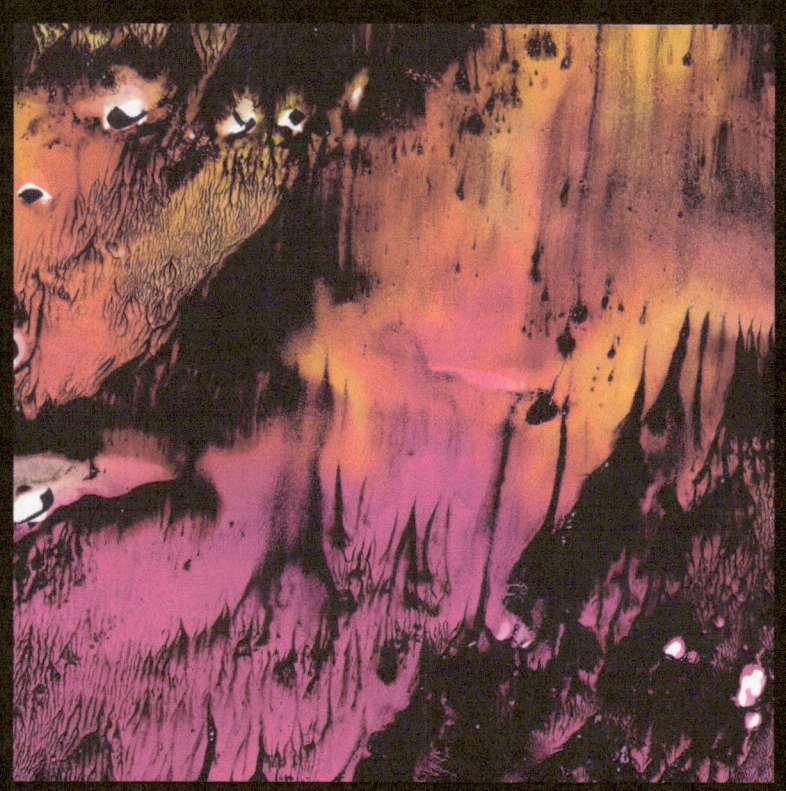

Va'aizek
Flame of fire

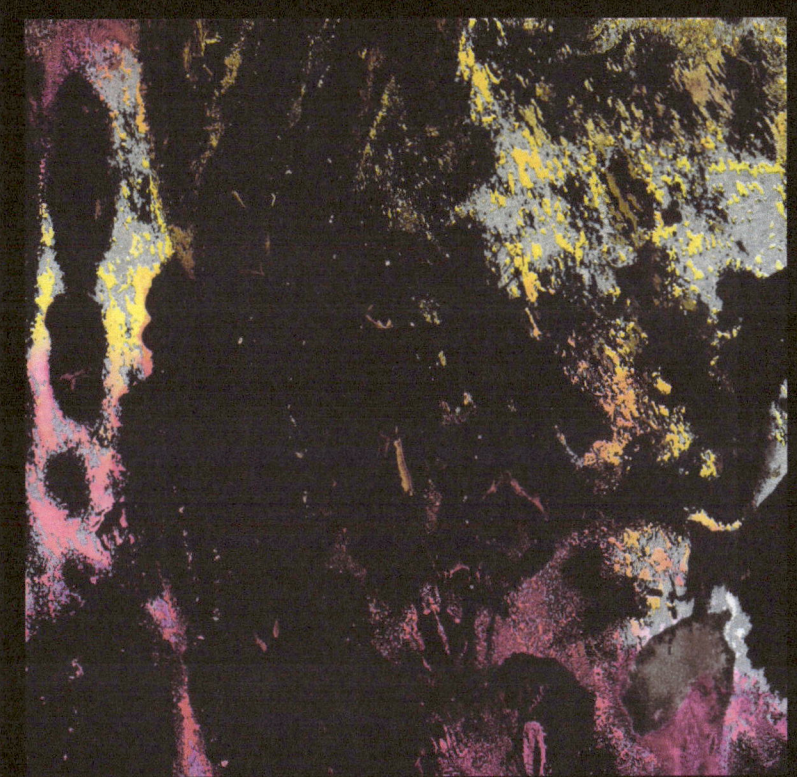

Na'aba'ai
Impossible

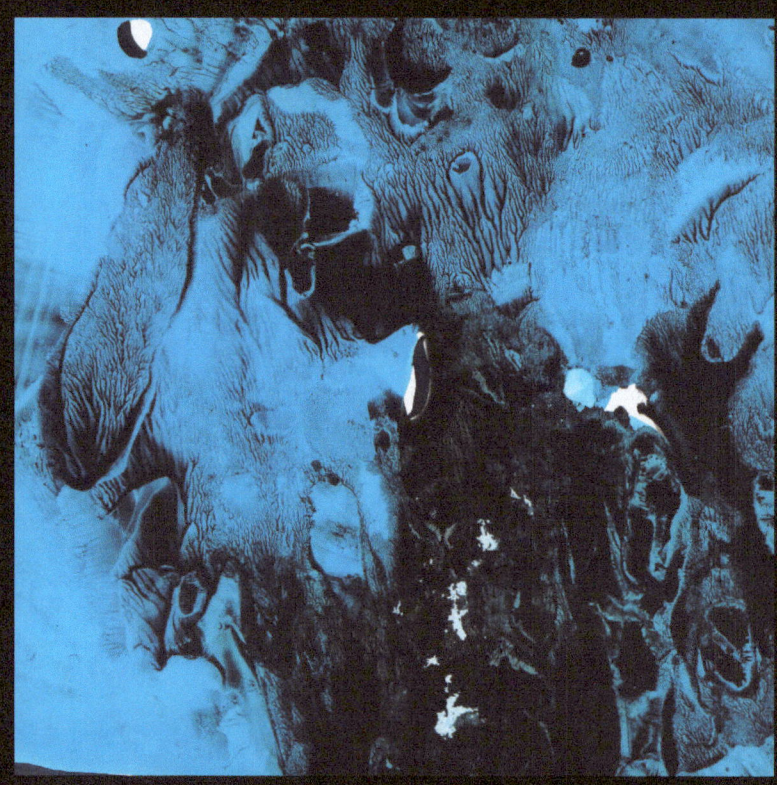

Madmad
River

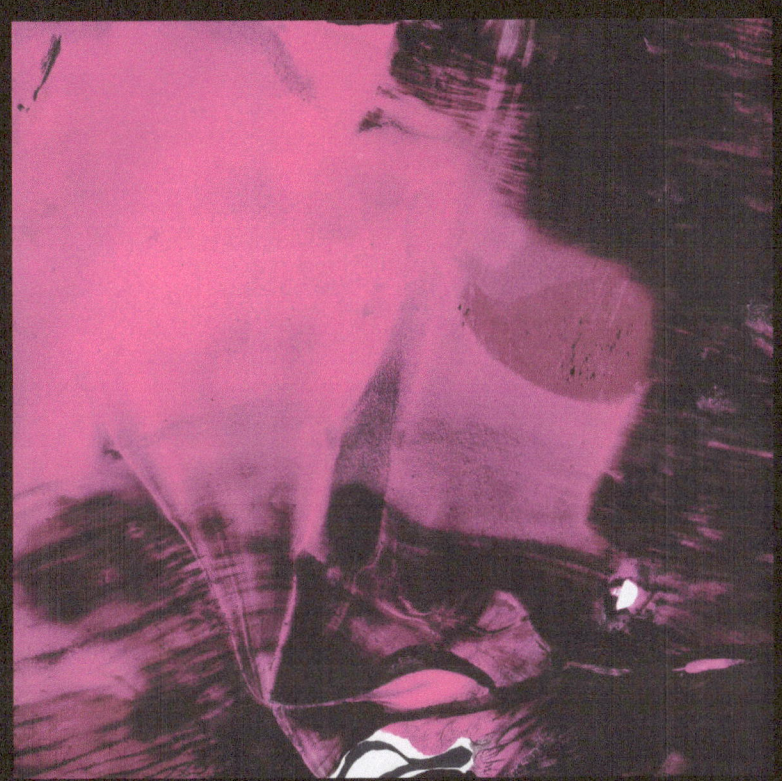

Shiraz A'al
Wine

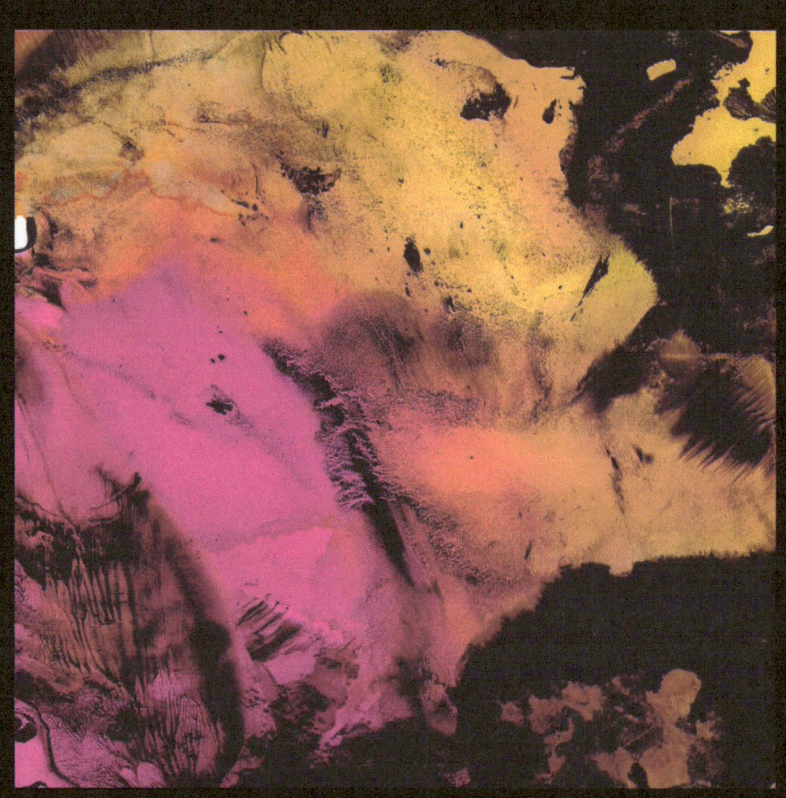

A'aseh
Dejection, withered

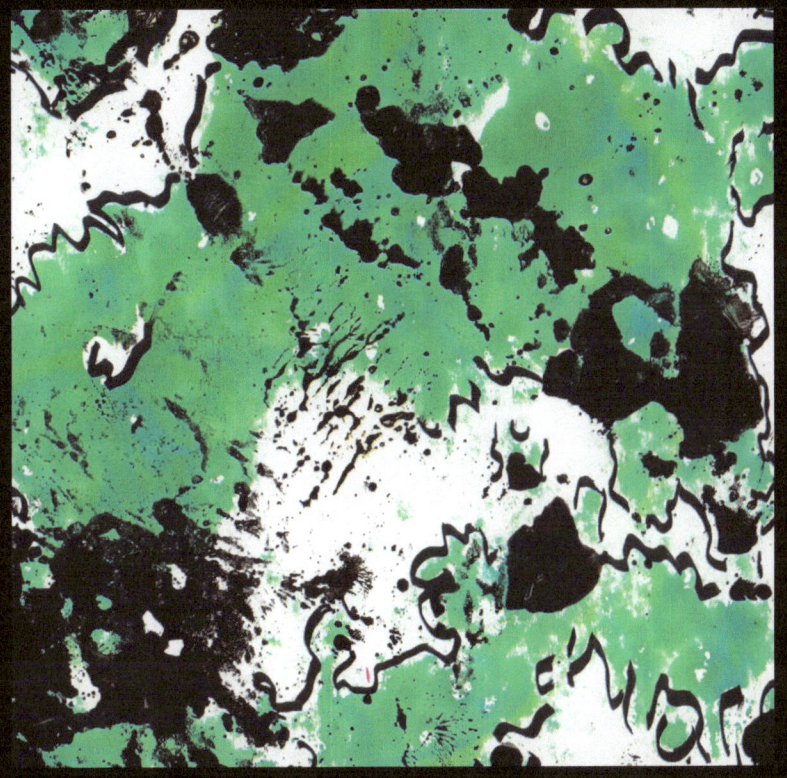

Daber
A green bird which pecks trees

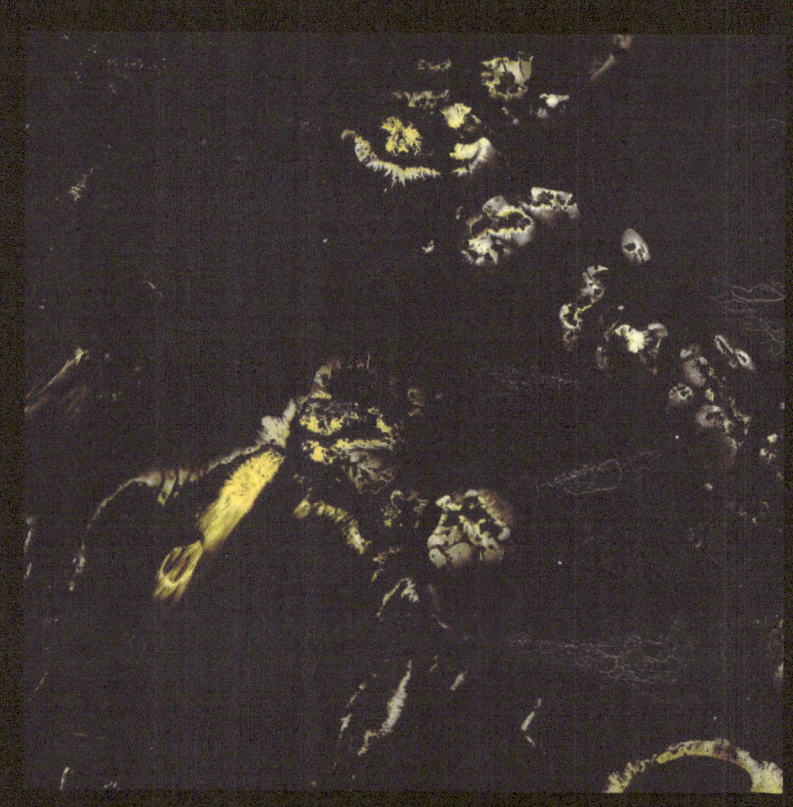

Sa'ar
A black, white spotted singing bird

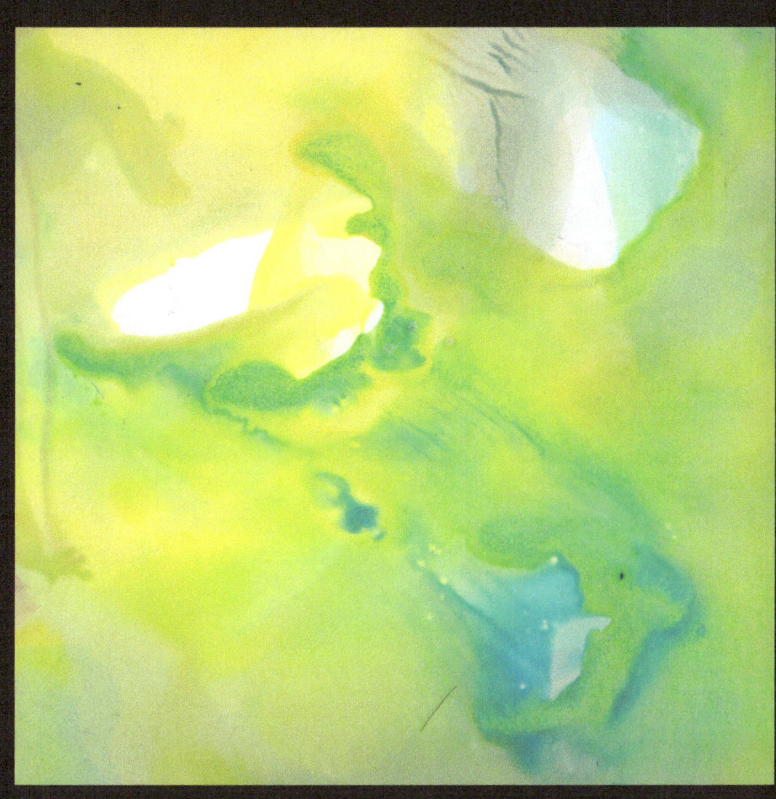

Solook
A mystic rite

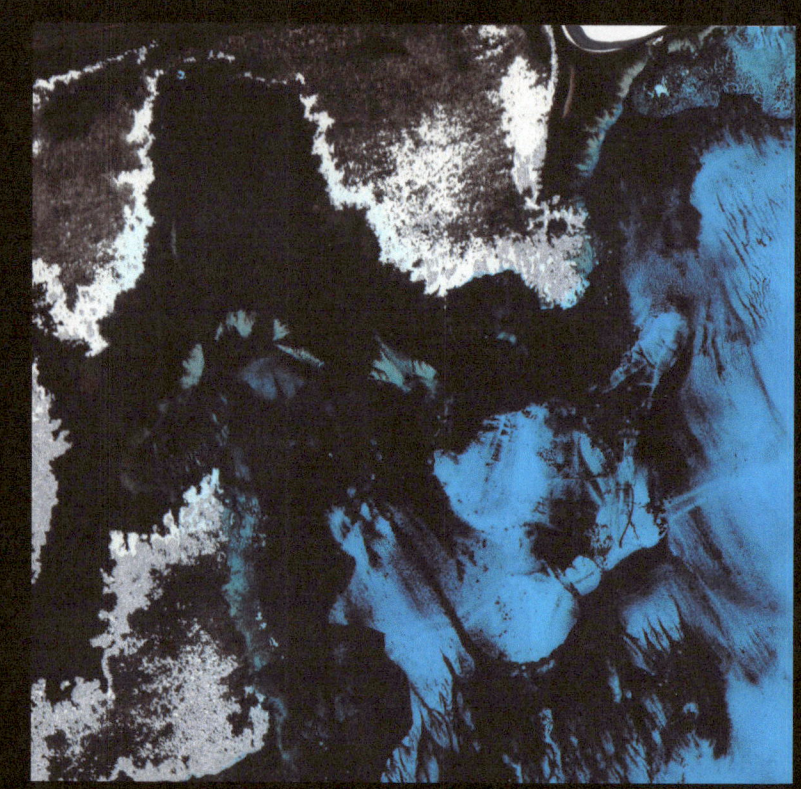

Yam
Sea

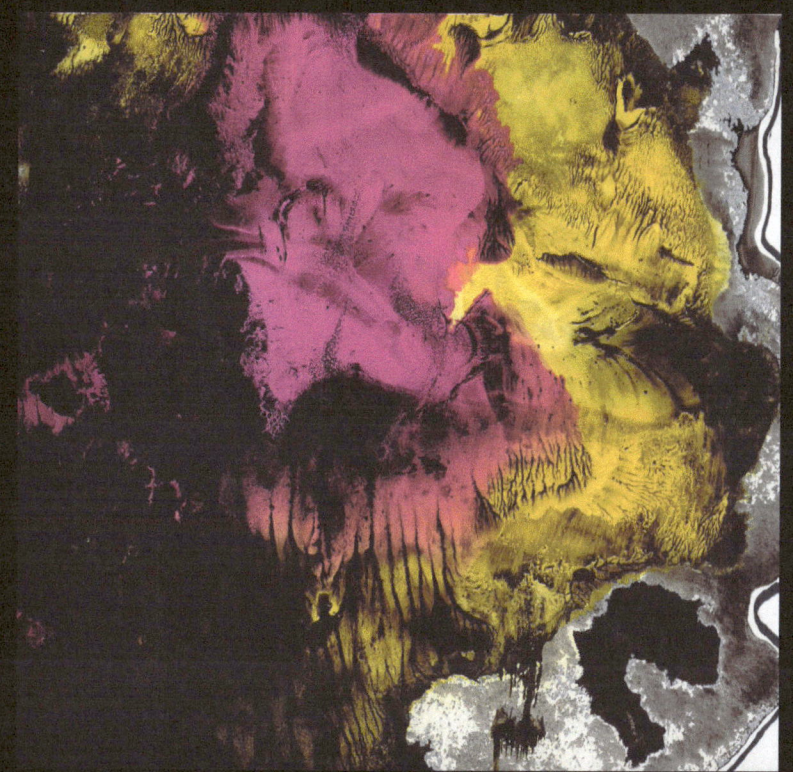

A'azar
Fire

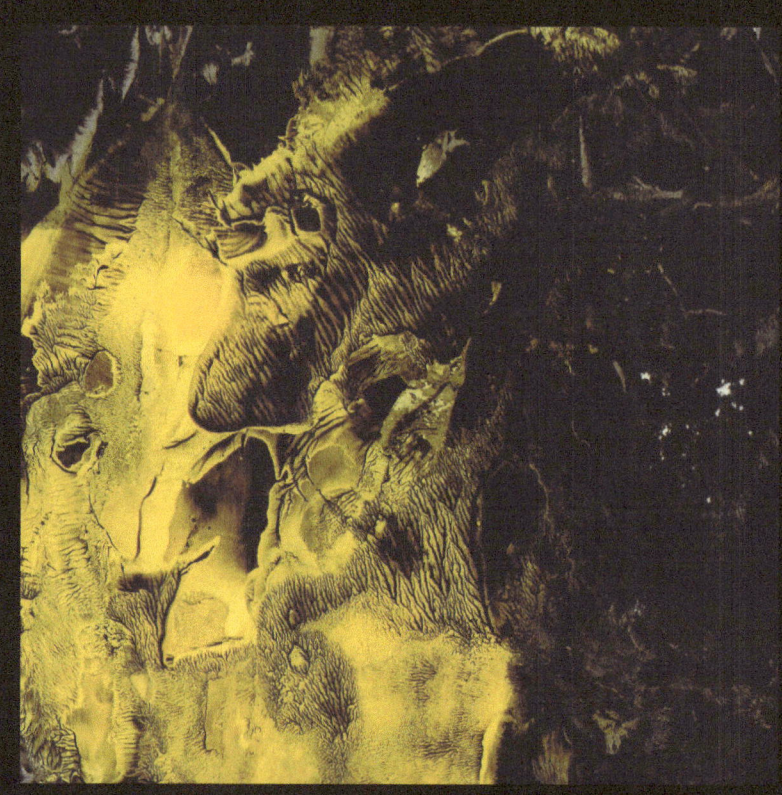

Da'amer
A yellow, gum-like substance

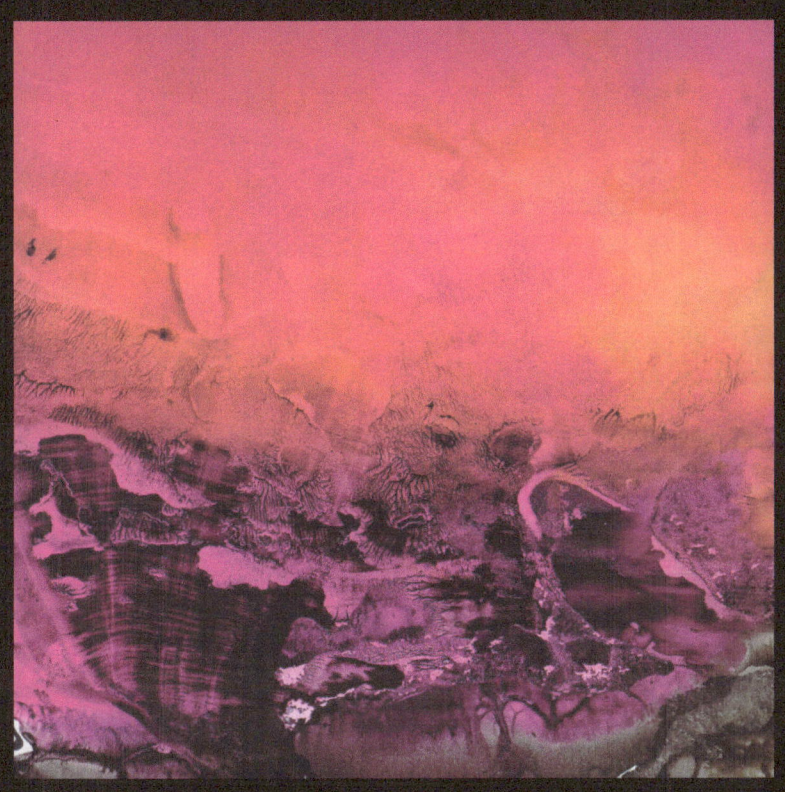

Saterka
A blackish red gum, olive tree gum

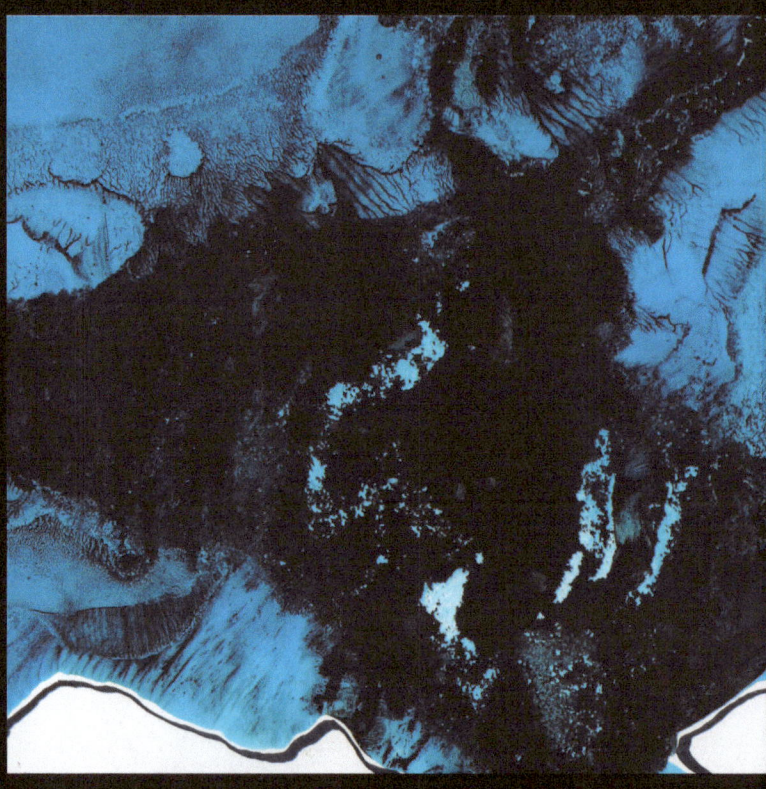

Cha'ala'ab
A pit filled with rain or flood

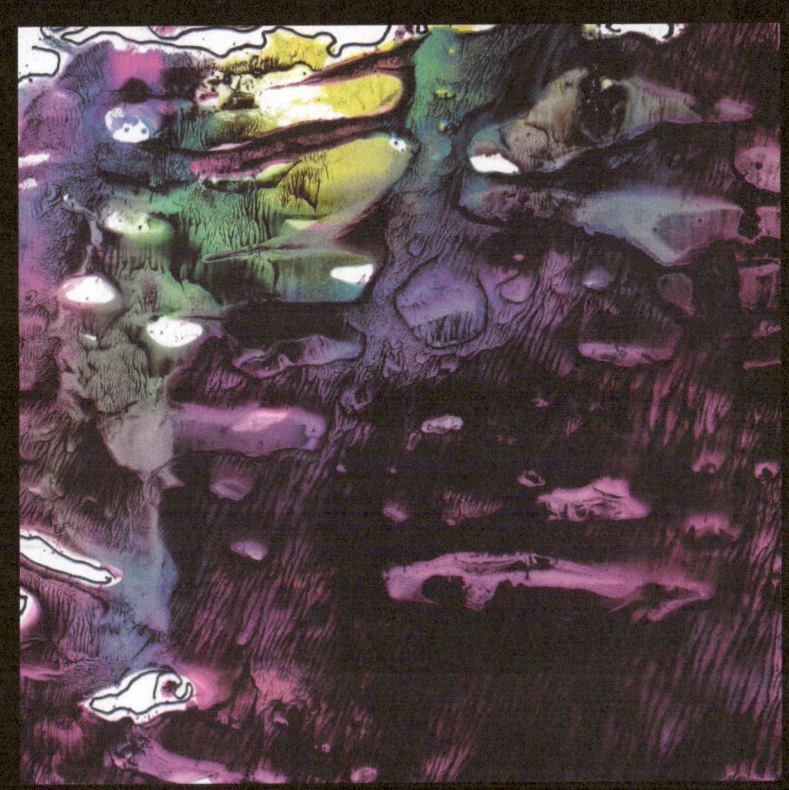

Afrang
Elegance

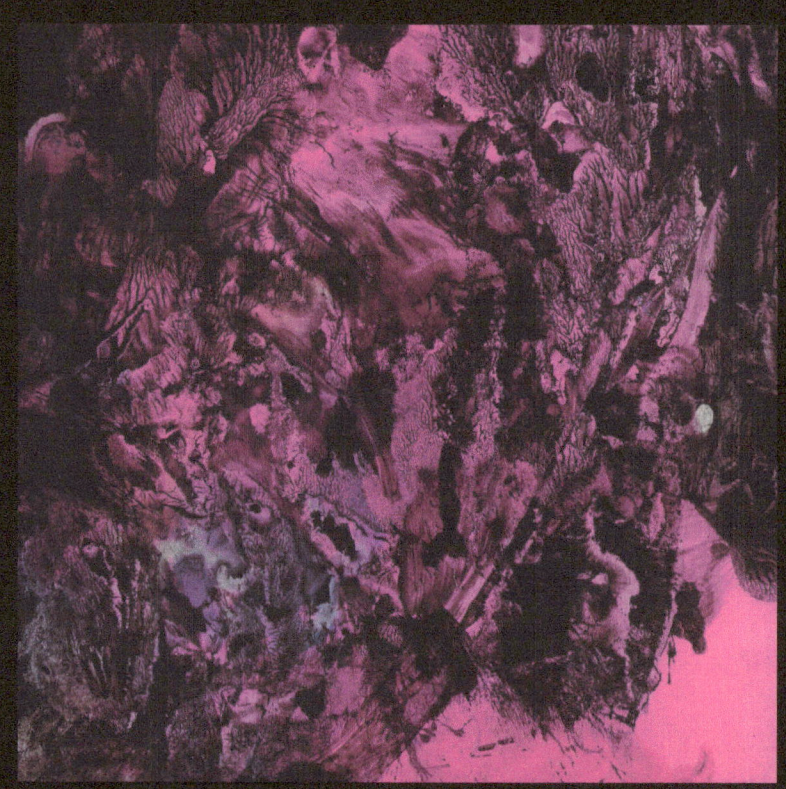

Ja'abiz
Flames of fire, tear of fire

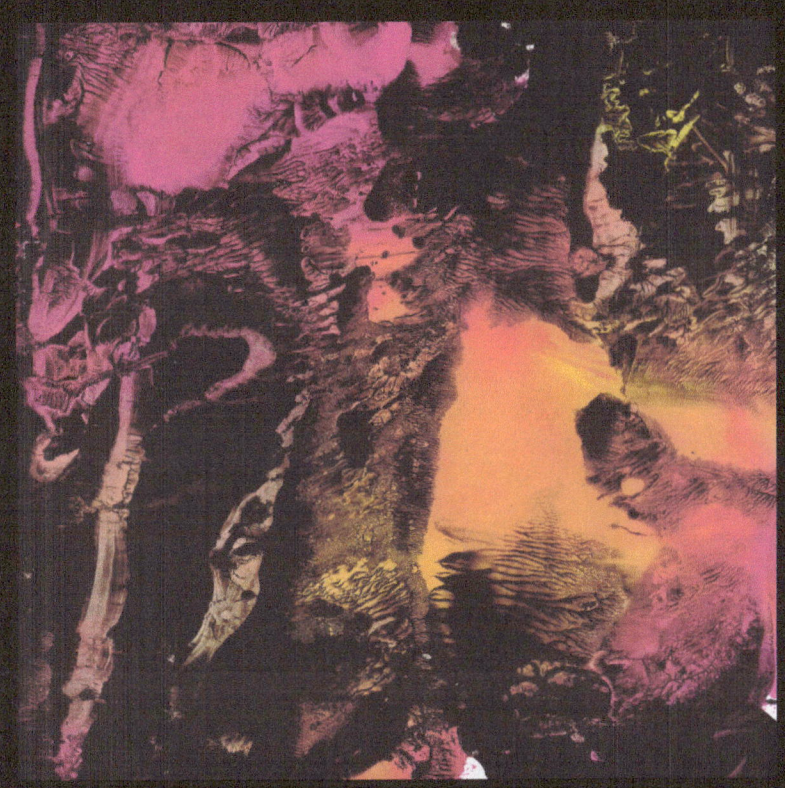

A'azargol
A red flower like Anemone

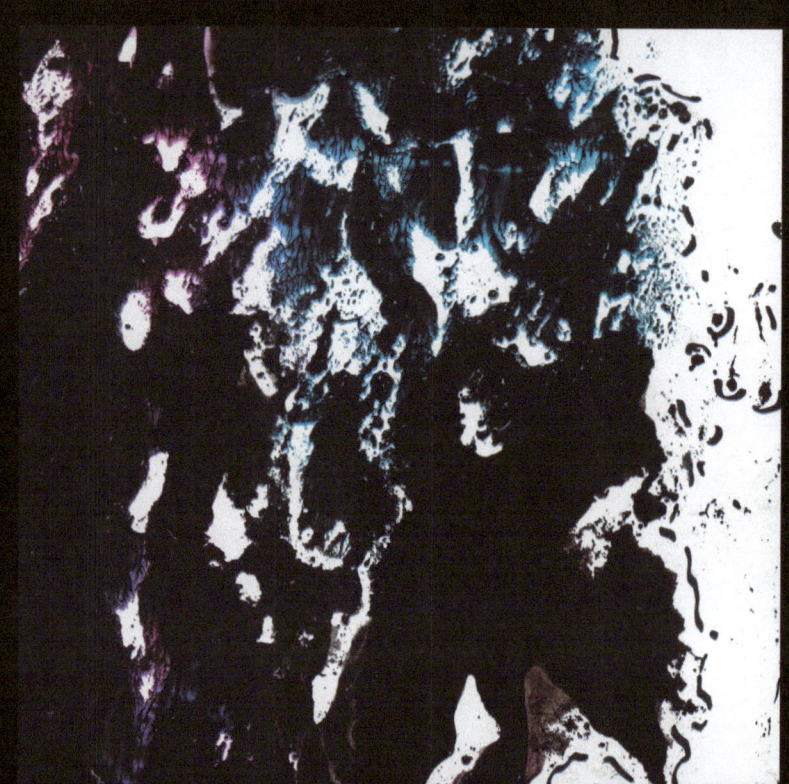

A'aderah
A cold night

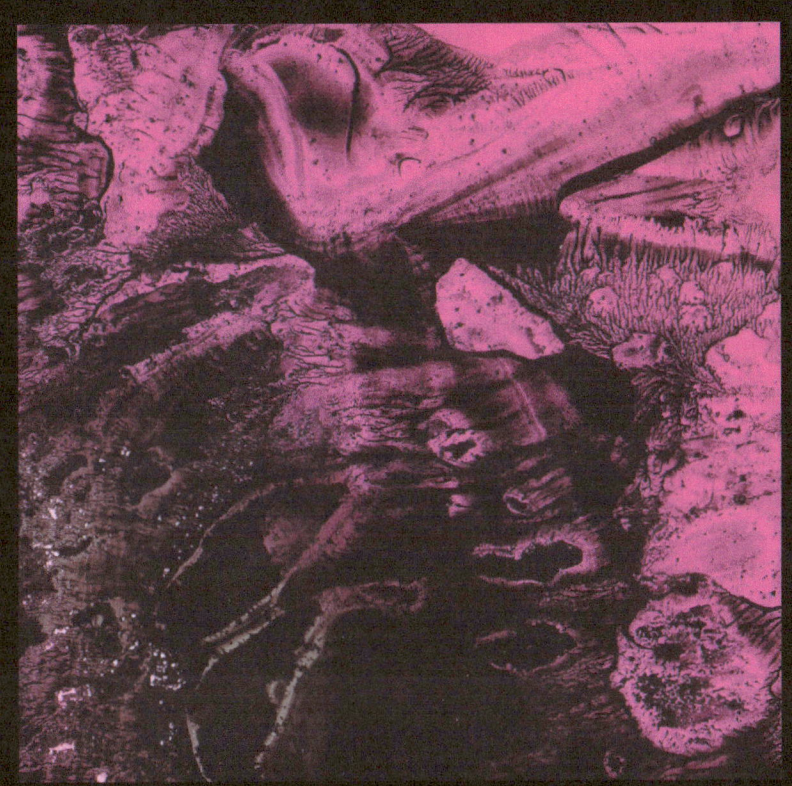

Sarta'ab
Rebellious

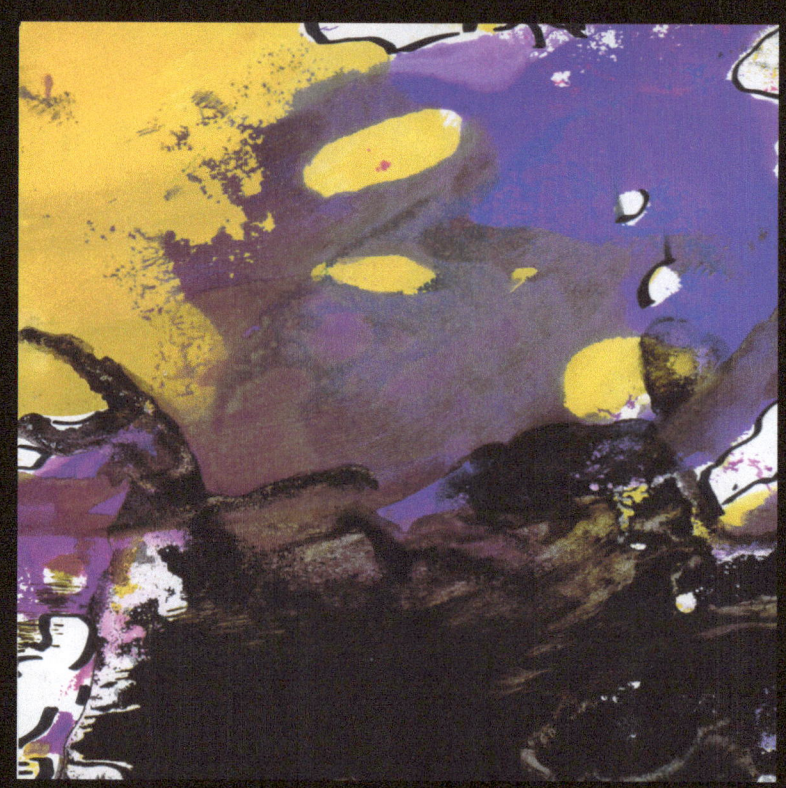

Ma'ab
Return

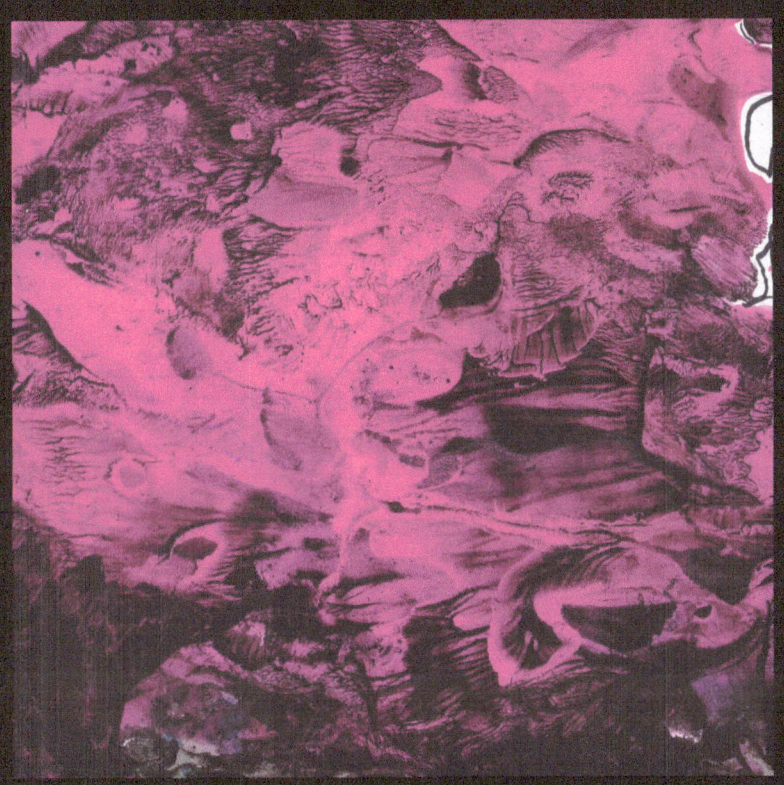

Rose essence
Wine

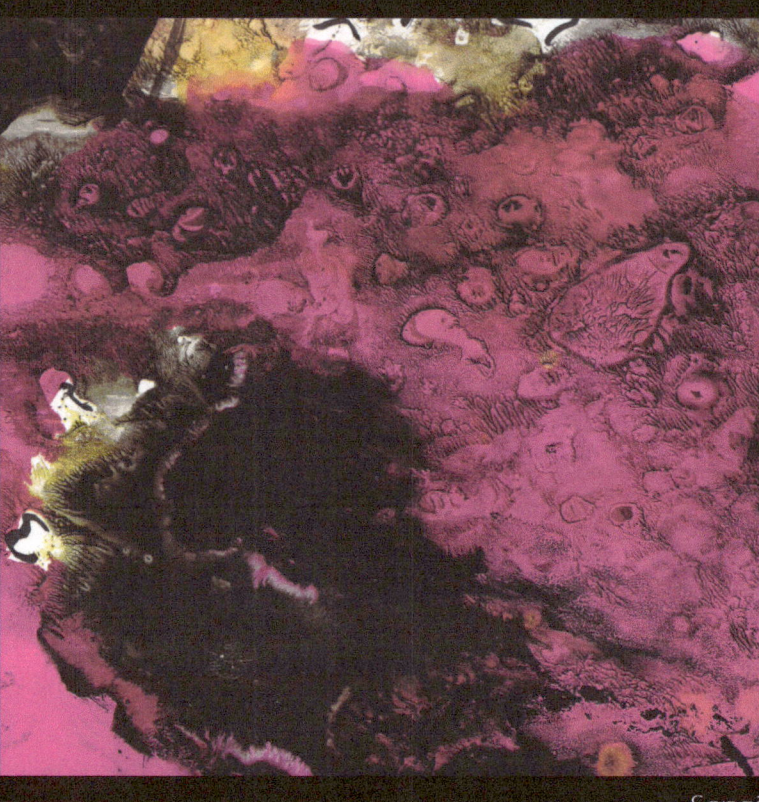

Senaj
Soot

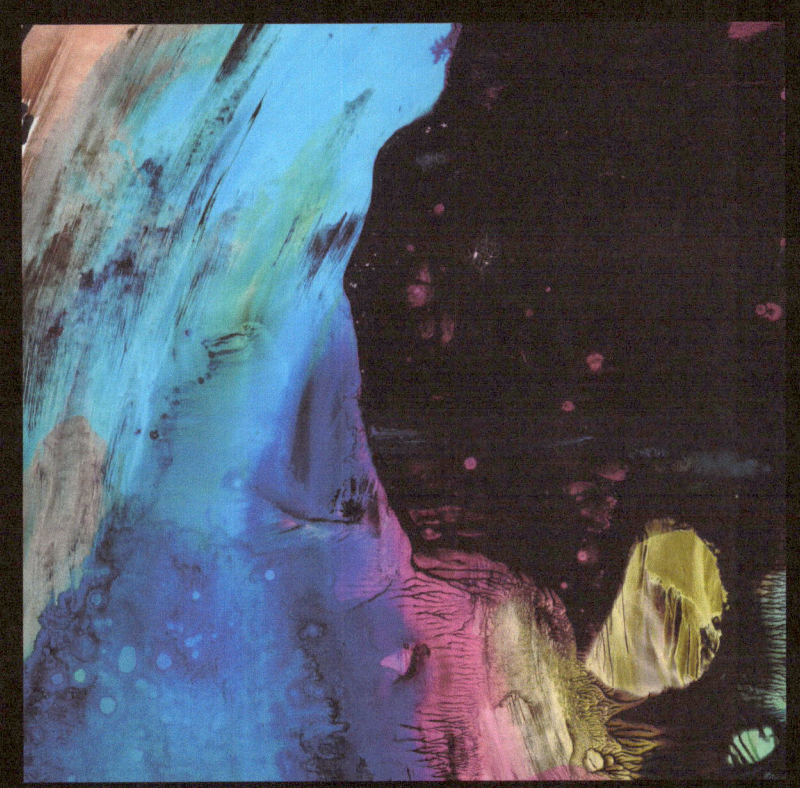

Masa'af
Distance

Ali Bazmandegan was born in Shiraz in 1983. He started painting portraits at the age of 20 and recently moved to a more abstract style. He experiments with different mediums till he finds the right combination for each painting. In 1999 Ali started working with metals creating sculptural pieces and that led him to designing interiors of commercial buildings. He continues to work in this manner.

www.alibazmandegan.com
instagram: a.b.studio
email: a.bazmandegan@gmail.com
phone: (0098)917 111 0128

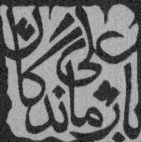

www.ingramcontent.com/pod-product-compliance
Lightning Source LLC
Chambersburg PA
CBHW050855180526
45159CB00007B/2681